ALL SHOOK UP

ALL SHOOK UP

Music, Passion, and Politics

CARSON HOLLOWAY

SPENCE PUBLISHING COMPANY • DALLAS
2001

Published in the United States by
Spence Publishing Company
111 Cole Street
Dallas, Texas 75207

Library of Congress Cataloging-in-Publication Data

Holloway, Carson, 1969-
    All shook up : music, passion, and politics / Carson Holloway
        p. cm.
    Includes bibliographical references and index.
    ISBN 1-890626-33-3 (alk. paper)
        1. Music—Political aspects.   2. Popular music—United States—Political aspects.   I. Title.
    ML3916.H65 2001
    306.4'84—dc21   00-047002

Printed in the United States of America

For my mother and my father

Contents

Acknowledgments

ONLY BY WRITING A BOOK have I come to understand the great extent to which the final product is the fruit of the efforts of many besides the author. This particular book began as my doctoral dissertation, written to satisfy the PH.D. requirements of the graduate program in political science at Northern Illinois University. I therefore owe many thanks to my dissertation director, Professor Gary D. Glenn, for suggesting to me the line of investigation I initially pursued and for his encouragement and advice during the writing of the dissertation. Much gratitude is also due to the other members of my dissertation committee, Professors Morton Frisch, Larry Arnhart, and Thomas Lindsay, all of whom also offered guidance from which I have profited immensely. Finally, I am very much beholden to Thomas Spence for his decision to publish my book and to Mitchell Muncy, my editor at Spence Publishing, whose judicious advice has proved invaluable.

The writing of the dissertation was supported in part by a Northern Illinois University Graduate School Dissertation Completion Award and by a University of Northern Iowa Frank Ivan Merchant Fellowship. The writing of chapters one, seven, and eight, by which the dissertation was transformed into the present book, was accomplished primarily over the summer of 1999, during which time my work was supported by an Earhart Foundation summer grant. Many thanks to all three of these institutions for their generous assistance.

In conclusion, I wish to thank my mother and father, as well as my mother- and father-in-law, without whose support, encouragement, and constant prayers this work would never have been completed. Finally, I owe very special thanks to my wife, Shari, not only for her encouragement and prayers but in addition for her generosity in enduring my long absences and shouldering the burden of caring first for little Maria and then the even littler Anna. All in all I had the much less demanding task.

Any virtue this book may possess could not have been achieved without the help of the people and institutions mentioned; any defects in it are strictly my own.

ALL SHOOK UP

For in rhythms and tunes there are likenesses particularly close to the genuine natures of anger and gentleness, and further of courage and moderation and of all the things opposite to these and of the other things pertaining to character. This is evident from the facts: we are altered in soul when we listen to such things.

Aristotle, *Politics*

So, Glaucon, I said, isn't this why the rearing in music is most sovereign? Because rhythm and harmony most of all insinuate themselves into the inmost part of the soul and most vigorously lay hold of it in bringing grace with them; and they make a man graceful if he is correctly reared, if not, the opposite.

Plato, *Republic*

1

Cultural Dissonance

M USIC IS A SIGN OF CONTRADICTION IN OUR CULTURE. We all feel that music is somehow of great importance. Almost everyone takes great joy in the music that suits his tastes, and hardly anyone would consent to a life deprived of music. Most people are inclined to defend their favorite music bitterly against criticism, let alone attempts to take it away from them. At the same time, we cannot seem to agree, with each other or even with ourselves, on why music is important and what it means for our society.

This cultural dissonance is reflected, in the first place, in our persistent arguments about the social significance of popular music, about its relationship to our desire for a decent and orderly society and to our aspirations for learning and the cultivation of the mind. Some, typically though not exclusively on the right, argue that much pop music encourages destructive behavior and ultimately threatens to undermine the moral foundations of the social order. Others, typically though not exclusively on the left, respond that such music is harmless or even helpful insofar as it brings to light social ills that need to be addressed. Our wise men, moreover, those who purport to understand the arts and their effect on us, are of no help in resolving this dispute because they themselves disagree on whether pop music undermines or assists the education of which they are the defenders and transmitters.

This lack of harmony also appears in the positions taken by the various parties to these disputes. Their arguments betray a lack of seriousness about music and a failure fully to come to grips with its power. Conservative critics of contemporary pop are satisfied by the omission of a few blatantly obscene lyrics, even though the spirit of the music remains the same. Pop's liberal defenders claim it is no big deal one way or the other, yet the very vehemence of their reaction to the critics suggests that it is somehow a very big deal indeed.

We need some account of music that can bring greater coherence and depth to our understanding, some wisdom in light of which we can judge our own music. This book seeks such wisdom in the tradition of political philosophy—which offers unequivocal support to neither side of the debate. Critic and defender, liberal and conservative, all utterly fail to grasp, first, the natural power of music itself—that is, music without words—to move the soul and, second, music's consequent ability to aid or impede not only our quest for a decent social order but also our striving for the goods in which we find our fullest happiness.

Popular Music and Popular Morality

It is perhaps impossible to identify a specific origin of the American concern with the effect of popular music on the character and behavior of young people. It has often, and probably rightly, been said that every generation of parents has grumbled about the musical tastes of its children. Grown-ups worried first about jazz, then about Elvis, then the Beatles, and many other musical phenomena since, sometimes to the consternation and sometimes to the amusement of the young people who like the music.

One can, however, identify a particular event that marks the be-

ginning of the more recent debate over the social and moral significance of contemporary popular music: the founding, in 1985, and rise
to prominence of the Parents' Music Resource Center (PMRC). The
organization was founded in the spring of that year by a (bipartisan)
group of spouses of important national politicians, the most prominent among them being Tipper Gore and Susan Baker, wife of James
Baker who at the time was Ronald Reagan's treasury secretary. The
"Washington wives," as they were often called by their detractors, were
spurred to action after hearing the music to which their own children
were listening. They called on the record industry to help parents,
by rating record albums, to restrict their children's access to potentially offensive music. Their campaign reached its climax in the fall
of 1985 in the celebrated hearing on this issue held by the Senate
Committee on Commerce, Science, and Transportation.

Despite all its confrontational drama, with the likes of Frank
Zappa and Dee Snyder going head to head with such as the Gores and
Senator Ernest Hollings, the hearings led only to a small change in
the practices of the music industry. The record companies ultimately
agreed to label potentially offensive material but did so with each
company deciding for itself—and according to its own, instead of
industry-wide, standards—which recordings would be stickered.[1]

A more important achievement of the PMRC was that it sparked a
public debate on the moral and social impact of certain forms of
popular music, which has continued for fifteen years. Though wor-
ries about pop music had been around for a long time before 1985,
prior to the PMRC's campaign they were not of such continuous and
widespread concern. Its efforts brought to light significant changes
in popular music: now the messages about sex, drugs, and even violence were no longer veiled but vivid and vulgar, and their purvey-
ors were no longer marginal but among the most popular of rock
groups. Seemingly without the nation's grown-ups noticing, mainstream rock had changed much for the worse by 1985.

Since then, American popular music, or at least the music at the center of the controversy, has progressed so far that the music decried by the PMRC in 1985 now seems almost benign. Although some of the songs criticized at the time seemed to glorify violence, on the whole they were characterized chiefly by an infantile sexuality. While the depravity of such music no doubt warrants public protest, the alarming fact is that since 1985 violence has loomed larger and larger as a theme of popular music. Sex and violence, which in more innocent times one could safely assume to be distinct categories of obscenity, seem to have merged. Certain popular rock and rap acts sing not only about the joys of sex but of sex that is degrading or physically injurious to women.[2]

This increasingly rapid flight from even the most minimal standards of decency has led to two noteworthy changes in the public argument regarding the morality of popular music. First, politicians have shown greater boldness in confronting the issue. In 1985 the senators simply responded to a campaign spearheaded by women who were in many cases their own wives. But in recent years presidential candidates of both parties have, without prompting from others, raised the issue, indicating that they sense a growing public concern about such matters.

Second, as certain strains of popular music have become more aggressively unwholesome, new activists have emerged with more aggressive demands. The PMRC was always careful to point out that it was asking only that record companies provide the information parents need to make informed decisions, not demanding that they stop the production or distribution of such music. The activists of the 1990s, in contrast, have found some music so offensive that they have brought pressure on the music industry not to release it at all. This increased assertiveness has in turn provoked the defenders of pop music, and the debate has grown even more spirited.

The Critics' Case

The critics of pop music worry that it coarsens or degrades our culture, fearing that the unrestrained lust and hate which are the themes of choice in the music in question encourage large numbers of people to believe that such feelings are acceptable and perhaps even praiseworthy. More particularly, these critics fear that the effects of such music may be permanent, that it will leave a lasting impression on the character of the young people who imbibe it.

Much of the rhetoric advanced in defense of pop music suggests that its production and consumption is of no concern to anyone but the producers and consumers themselves. The critics are asked what difference it makes to them what kind of music other people like, and they are reminded that if such music offends them they are free not to buy it. Thus judgments about music are implicitly relegated to the private realms of taste and free economic exchange.

Nevertheless, the critics' invocation of culture is meant to suggest that the popularity of such music is decidedly a public concern. After all, by "the culture" they emphatically mean "popular culture" or "public culture." Thus their rhetoric implies that in influencing the culture such music is doing something to all of us, something that many of us do not want done.

Yet how can this be a tenable position in a liberal democracy? The defenders of pop music have a powerful point. After all, though the critics may disapprove of such music, and though they may be sincerely alarmed at the effect they fear that music will have on the thoughts and feelings of others, the notion that people's thoughts and feelings should be a matter of public concern is highly suspect in our society. Surely actions alone are of public concern, while thoughts and feelings belong to the private realm.

Critics of pop music respond that musical cultural pollution most emphatically is of public concern because it powerfully influences the

way people act. Many of the young devotees of such music, the argument goes, are influenced to behave in the way the music describes
and apparently recommends, and the result is the growth of social
pathologies that do significant material harm to society. Thus, such
music is not merely a private matter of what some people like in contrast to what others do not but a public matter of how large numbers
of people behave, and perhaps even of how a majority of tomorrow's
adults reared on today's popular music will behave. Pop music raises
serious concerns about the ultimate public and cultural question:
What kind of a people are we to be?

It is in this light that the critics go so far as to worry that this
music threatens the very survival of our civilization. Thus, for example, John Leo suggests that the "future" of our "free society" hangs
upon how we respond to pornographic pop music.[3] While such concerns may seem hyperbolic, the (usually unstated) arguments behind
them are reasonable on their face: A free society requires citizens with
the ability and willingness to exercise self-control. In the absence of
the public order such citizens support, coercion by the government
becomes necessary. Music that permanently undermines the capacity for self-control of large numbers of citizens is, in the long run,
destructive of our political freedom.

In Defense of Pop

Defenders of pop music have advanced a number of arguments
against this critique.* Critics wildly exaggerate the prevalence of obscene popular music, they contend, and pop music is for the most part
nothing more than harmless, if admittedly mindless, fun. If the

---

    * I refer with some reservation to the "defenders" of pop music. The term can
be misleading if one does not bear in mind that some of these defenders de-
plore pop music, but still oppose efforts to restrict it. Thus, they are defenders
of this music only in the sense of being defenders, they would say, of the freedom of those who produce and consume it.

themes of some pop tunes are offensive, the defenders add, it is not a problem because kids pay no attention to the words anyway.

Additionally, some hold that even when obscene lyrics are present, heard, and understood, they do not cause the harmful behaviors the critics fear. One author asserts, for example, that "the cause and effect link between rap music and violence is weak. For every scholar who offers research that the link exists, another will offer research to dispute the claim."[4] Similarly, Robert Pattison, in a penetrating account of rock music to which I will turn presently, contends that "rock is a mythical phenomenon with little direct effect on ordinary behavior" and that "any connection between rock mythology and the behavior of large numbers of people is unproven and probably unprovable." Indeed, the "advantage of a mythic system of belief is" precisely "that it allows the believer" to "live a full emotional life inside the myths" instead of "in the danger of external events."[5]

This argument has even received unexpected support from the political and cultural right. Writing in *First Things*, music professor Michael Linton downplays the moral and ethical influence of his art. Music, he contends, "can never cause the listener to act" because "action is always a function of the will," which music cannot overpower. Thus, a "lifetime spent listening to Bach will not automatically make a woman love God. And—despite the warnings of two generations of moralists—a lifetime listening to the Rolling Stones will not make a man fornicate."[6]

Another approach frequently employed by the defenders of pop music is to speak of its significance as art. Moving the debate into this rhetorical territory provides the basis for two arguments. In the first place, it makes plausible the suggestion that the harsh exterior of some songs may not be the true substance of the music, that a benign or at least harmless content may lurk beneath the gritty surface. On this argument, concern over the content of pop music is often based on mere misunderstanding: what moralistic critics take as obscenity is often no more than artistic convention. Hence, Ice-T's

"Cop Killer" is merely "one more entry in pop music's long history of macho hyperbole and violent boast," and the detractors of heavy metal rock have mistakenly "literalized" its "theatrical excessiveness."[7]

Alternatively, discussion of pop music as art allows it to be defended even when its fundamental message clearly is obscene and brutal. Such a defense rests on the notion that art's function is to depict reality, even, and especially when, reality is grim. Thus the music of gansta rap group N.W.A. is said to communicate "vital information about the urban front lines," to offer a chronicle of the "daily horrors of life in South Central L.A." that "poses a moral and political challenge to anyone who encounters it."[8]

The presentation of such music as a form of realist art communicating politically relevant information about the plight of the underclass also allows its defenders to go on the offensive against the critics. Hence the frequent portrayal of the critique of gansta rap as a class-based power play, an attempt by the friends of oppressive authority to silence the voices of the downtrodden. On this view, "Cop Killer" is "so shocking" because "in postliberal America, black anger is virtually taboo," and the furor such music provokes arises purely from the perception it is a threat "to the white power structure" it condemns.[9]

Finally, and most frequently, the defenders of pop music raise the specter of censorship. This line of argument was among the first advanced in 1985, and it has been a prominent part of the debate ever since. Organized opposition to what some take to be offensive music, the defenders contend, either amounts to, or will quickly lead to, official regulation of thought and speech. Hence Time Warner's defense of its sponsorship of violent rap: "We stand for creative freedom. We believe that the worth of what an artist or journalist has to say does not depend on preapproval from a government official or a corporate censor."[10]

Rock's Closed-Mindedness

In addition to the familiar dispute over the moral and social impact of popular music there has been another debate, not less important, about rock music's relationship to the life of the mind, to liberal education or education in the humanities. This controversy arises from the arguments of two books by two distinguished scholars, Allan Bloom and Robert Pattison. Bloom's *The Closing of the American Mind* and Pattison's *The Triumph of Vulgarity: Rock Music in the Mirror of Romanticism* were published in the same year, 1987, and therefore do not address each other directly. Nevertheless, they offer such profoundly different accounts of what rock music can contribute to liberal education that a controversy can be said to exist between the books, even if it did not exist between the authors.

The Closing of the American Mind, of course, addresses far more than rock music. It offers an account of an entire climate of thought, dominant both in the academy and in society at large, that Bloom finds to be incompatible with the serious study of ideas. Yet the book's immense fame owes much to its discussion of—in fact to a widespread misunderstanding of—Bloom's account of rock. Since *The Closing of the American Mind* appeared only two years after the PMRC started the national conversation about the impact of pop music on the character of the young, many who read it, or who read about it, assumed that Bloom condemned rock music primarily on moral grounds. It was not uncommon for hostile reviewers to place Bloom in the political and cultural company of the "religious right" or for cultural conservatives to assume that in Bloom they had found a scholar who shared their concerns.

Indeed, at first sight there does appear to be a certain kinship between Bloom and the moralistic critics of rock. Much of Bloom's account breathes a disdain for pop music that the moralists would surely approve. He ridicules the typical rock star as a "drag queen," derisively refers to Mick Jagger's "tarting it up on stage," and labels the music of such pop stars of the 1980s as Prince, Boy George, and the more durable Michael Jackson as a "gutter phenomenon." In addition, his remarks sometimes betray a belief that such music is morally harmful and socially destructive, as when he asserts in passing the idea that rock "dissolves the beliefs and morals necessary for a liberal society."[11]

Nevertheless, Bloom explicitly states that his concern "is not with the moral effects of this music—whether it leads to sex, violence, or drugs," but with its "effect on education," specifically its power to incapacitate the young for the pursuit of humane learning. Rock music, he contends, "ruins the imagination of young people and makes it very difficult for them to have a passionate relationship to the art and thought that are the substance of liberal education."[12]

Rock addresses the young at that stage in their development that is crucial in determining their character. The earliest "sensuous experiences," Bloom argues, are "decisive in determining the taste for the whole of life." Therefore, the "period of nascent sensuality has always been used for sublimation," for "making sublime" our "youthful inclinations and longings" by connecting them "to music, pictures and stories that provide the transition to the fulfillment of the human duties and the enjoyment of the human pleasures." In other words, the education we receive, and especially the music we hear, at this formative stage should prepare the way for liberal education or the cultivation of the pleasures of the mind, the truly human pleasures of which Blooms speaks, by directing the emerging passions of the young toward the noble and the beautiful, the proper objects of liberal study. Immersion in the right kind of music should be "at the center" of the education of the young, "both for giving the passions their due and for preparing the soul for the unhampered use of reason."[13]

Rock music, however, does not sublimate the budding desires of youth by directing them toward lofty objects that transcend the stirrings and satisfactions of the flesh. Instead, Bloom argues, rock directs youthful sexual longing only toward sex itself, sex shorn of any association with the noble or beautiful. Rock, he famously asserts, "has one appeal only, a barbaric appeal, to sexual desire—not love, not *eros*, but sexual desire undeveloped and untutored. It acknowledges the first emanations of children's emerging sensuality and addresses them seriously, eliciting them and legitimizing them." Thus rock powerfully impresses on people in their most impressionable period of life the lesson that sex and nothing else is the fulfillment of human longing, and thus it cuts them off forever from any serious dedication to the pursuits of the mind. Hence Bloom's memorable conclusion to his account of music: "As long as they have the walkman on, they cannot hear what the great tradition has to say. And, after its prolonged use, when they take it off, they find they are deaf."[14]

The Virtues of Vulgarity

Pattison agrees fundamentally with Bloom about the character of rock music. The first point on which they concur is that rock music has a definable character. Against those who contend that rock embraces a variety of styles expressing a diversity of sentiments and thoughts, Pattison, like Bloom, thinks that rock music stands for something, monolithically. The nature of rock, he argues, can be gleaned from an analysis of its lyrics, which, repeatedly evincing the same themes, reveal the "world of thought in which the rocker lives." Rock, therefore, "distinguishes itself from all other music by a shared ideology that crosses all its internal divisions."[15]

Rock's nature is, in a word, vulgarity, understood in contradistinction to refinement. Vulgarity, says Pattison, is not so much a positive presence as it is privation, specifically the "absence of cultivation." It is the realm of "ordinary men without education." Reason plays a key role in the life of the refined. The refined man uses reason to rise above "the world as it appears to the unaided sense," ascending to the contemplation of some transcendent reality. Then, when he comes down to earth again, the refined man uses the transcendent as a standard by which to make reasoned distinctions about the world of the senses, judging some experiences and pleasures to be more elevated and others more base. In contrast, the vulgarian is characterized by his pantheism: for him, the world of the senses is all there is. As he is unaware or unconvinced of the existence of the transcendent, "common language, common activity, common sensation are the be-all and end-all of" the vulgarian's existence. Moreover, in the absence of the transcendent as a standard of judgment, rational evaluation of sensual experience must be utterly alien to vulgarity. Hence, the vulgarian "cannot discriminate between sensations," and as a result sensation itself comes to the fore as his standard of judgement.[16]

Rock is, for Pattison, characterized chiefly by its wholehearted embrace of vulgarity thus understood. Deeply indebted to romanticism's belief in man as fundamentally a passionate being, rock teaches that "man in his native state is indeed a willful animal and that in his naked desire lies his highest nobility." As a result, "rock lyrics are suffused with the language of emotion; *need*, *want*, and *feel* are the building blocks of its abstract vocabulary," and it takes such words with great seriousness. Thus, despite rock's claim to have arisen from the blues, its character differs decisively from that of the older and, to Pattison's mind, less vulgar genre. While rock deals with many of the same themes as the blues, sex and alcohol prominent among them, it approaches them all with a "passionate intensity" that naturally follows from its intellectual confinement to the realm of mere sensation and is far removed from the detachment and irony of the blues. Thus, for example, rock's account of sex is invariably "tumid and immediate" while that of the blues is frequently "fretsome and amusing."[17]

Moreover, rock's elevation of passion and desire, their establishment as the deepest ground of human nature, is necessarily accompanied by the "subordination of reason to feeling." Thus rock "insists" that "consciousness, reason, and mind" are "secondary qualities, that we know the universe first by feeling, and without feeling, we don't know it at all." According to rock ideology, "thought is only valid when ratified by sensation."[18]

Finally, rock's elevation of feeling over reason leads to its rejection of traditional Western education, which, in seeking to cultivate the life of the mind as something inherently good, reveals itself as a manifestation of refinement that is unacceptable to rock's militant vulgarity. Thus rock's "exaggerated hostility to education" flows naturally from its "romantic commitment to instinct." If desire is at the center of human nature, then the pursuit of reason in an attempt to transcend desire must result in a kind of sickness of the spirit, a withering of the soul. Rock associates "logic and reason" with "the loss of youth and the death of vitality" and presents "contemporary white civilization" as "effete, sterile, and impotent," producing human beings that are "overeducated and undersexed, unnatural and inauthentic."[19]

There is, then, substantial agreement between Bloom and Pattison on both the nature of rock and its relationship to the traditional humanities. While Bloom presents rock as being primarily about sex and Pattison characterizes it more broadly as elevating desire generally, still they concur in thinking that this music is committed to passion as opposed to reason. Moreover, both believe that rock is hostile to the traditional pursuit of the liberal arts, though they arrive at this conclusion differently, Pattison's approach being more theoretical and Bloom's more psychological. The former points out that rock's ideology is incompatible with the pursuit of the refinements of mind as good in themselves, while the latter argues that rock's catering to the immature sexuality of the young renders them unable to feel any longing for the objects of liberal study.

The crucial way in which Bloom and Pattison differ is in their evaluation of rock's nature and its relation to the humanities. In the conflict between rock and liberal education that both perceive, Bloom and Pattison have opposing loyalties. For Bloom rock is a bad thing because it incapacitates the young for liberal education, the pursuit of which Bloom believes to be the highest happiness human beings can achieve. In contrast, Pattison sides with rock against the traditional study of the humanities and its defenders. As *The Triumph of Vulgarity* draws to its close, Pattison remarks that the American "cultural community has responded" to the vulgar energies of rock "with innovative acts of suicidal ingratitude, exemplified by the report on college education prepared by President Reagan's secretary of education." Pattison then quotes a passage from the report in which William Bennett, following Matthew Arnold, defines the humanities in terms of "the best that has been said, thought, written, and otherwise expressed about the human condition," a formulation with which Bloom would no doubt agree. Pattison, however, dismisses this as so much "vacuous posturing" displaying an "airy reverence" for a European model of culture that stresses refinement of mind and the pursuit of the transcendent and is therefore irrelevant to the members of a democratic society that "thrives on vulgarity." "If this describes the humanities," says Pattison, "no wonder so few American students give a damn about them."[20]

In order better to appreciate Pattison's position, it is helpful to reconsider the title of his book: *The Triumph of Vulgarity*. For Pattison, rock's vulgarity is the perfect expression of the democratic spirit. Democracy, after all, is rule by men who lack a refined education, who are unconcerned with the transcendent, common men who live in the realm of common experience and common sensation. As Aristotle observed, the rulers set the tone of society, and where the vulgar rule society's dominant tastes will be vulgar. The final victory of vulgarity in America against the dwindling remnant of the refined should come as no surprise. Pattison is convinced that failure is the inevitable result of any attempt to impose on American students a model of higher education that aims at refinement.

Pattison's attitude is "if you can't beat the vulgarians, join them." Instead of aligning ourselves with the likes of Bennett and Bloom, who bootlessly rage against the dying of the academic light, we should rather seek to erect a new liberal education on the basis of vulgarity itself. "Isn't it possible," Pattison asks, "a hundred years after Whitman and William James," the forerunners of rock's vulgarity, "for Americans to make a definition of the humanities based on their own vulgar pantheism?" Such humanities would presumably partake of the underappreciated, yet eminently democratic, virtues of vulgarity— and of rock—that Pattison identifies. Vulgarity may, from the perspective of traditional education, appear "abysmally indiscriminate," but it is necessarily at the same time "infinitely tolerant," leaving room for "the atheist and the witchdoctor as well as the pope and the rabbi." It might be "cheap," but that also means that "it appreciates life" as it is and "delights" in its "humble routines." It might be "selfish and sensuous," but this also means being "pragmatic and pleasant." It is frivolous, but it at least has "a sense of humor."[21]

Music and Politics

The disputes detailed above, these signs of cultural dissonance, point to our need for some source of musical wisdom in the light of which we might find a resolution. But where are we to seek such wisdom? Contemporary political science is of no help, for it is almost completely indifferent to, or perhaps even ignorant of, the cultural and political implications of music. This is true of both its empirical and normative branches. Aside from the occasional study of the use of jingles in campaign commercials, empirical political science says nothing on this topic. It is indeed largely indifferent to the questions of formation of character and refinement of mind in relation to which music might be seen to have public importance. Normative political theory, in touch with the history of political philosophy, is at least aware that some thinkers of the first rank have given serious attention to these issues. It has not, however, itself given much serious attention to their musical teaching, let alone sought in them an account that might be applied to the controversies of our day.

Here, then, we will turn for insight to the history of political philosophy. We will investigate the role that reflection on the political significance of music plays, both by its presence and its absence, in that history. We will examine seminal thinkers—Plato, Aristotle, Rousseau, and Nietzsche—who treat music with great seriousness, as well as others no less important—Hobbes, Locke, and Montesquieu— who barely discuss it at all. We will seek to understand both the differences in the manner in which music is treated among those who agree on its political importance and the differences between those who treat music as a serious political concern and those who do not.

The debate over music is, in essence, a debate over the place of reason and passion in human nature, their proper relationship to each other in the soul, and the proper relationship of both to politics. The ancients, Plato and Aristotle, asserting the primacy of reason, seek to use music to calm the passions with a view to the noble rule of reason in the soul and the city. Hobbes, Locke, and Montesquieu, the early moderns, convinced of the priority of passion, dispense with music, aiming for a low but decent politics in which reason serves, rather than rules, the passions. The later critics of modernity, Rousseau and Nietzsche, accepting the priority of passion but also seeing a need to reinvogorate it, resurrect the power of music, aiming to use it to inflame the passions and silence reason in the service of a new, more noble politics.

Some may doubt at the outset that an inquiry into such a debate could possibly be relevant to current issues. Are not all these thinkers members of that frequently maligned, and even more frequently ignored, group, the Dead, White, European, Males? Surely their thought, ranging from one hundred to nearly twenty-five hundred years old, is outmoded, inapplicable to the modern controversies that we have been discussing.

Ultimately, the proof of the book is in the reading. Whether such an investigation can shed any useful light on these contemporary issues can only be known once we have tried to do it, and that requires reading the book to its end. Nevertheless, we can briefly offer some reasons for thinking that such an enterprise might prove valuable.

We may point first to the usefulness of taking our case before a panel of disinterested judges. The controversy over music's social significance has given rise to intensely felt political passions. The participants are divided into two hostile camps, each perceiving that dearly held interests and principles depend on winning the argument. Such a situation is not conducive to an impartial consideration of the issues. Hence, we are more likely to gain an enlightened appreciation for the true merits of the arguments advanced by turning for instruction to those who, by their very distance in time from the prevailing controversy, have no stake in the conflict. Simply put, if we want to come nearer the truth about these issues, we need to turn to the partisans of the truth about politics, the political philosophers. This is no claim that the political philosophers I examine in this book possess the truth about music's relationship to politics. It would be silly to say that, especially in light of their serious disagreements on so many important questions surrounding the issue. The point is that these political philosophers are likely to be a useful guide insofar as their primary interest is in understanding things as they really are, rather than vindicating this or that partisan position.

Second, the thinkers studied here are likely to be useful teachers because of their distance, not only from our intensely felt differences, but also from our unacknowledged—because unsuspected—agreements. It may be the case that our fierce differences over music and culture conceal agreement on important matters, which is unacknowledged because it never occurs to anyone that they could be debated. They represent the common sense of society, accepted by virtually all its members. In other words, such agreements represent opinions about the nature of politics and the good society so widely and unreflectively held that they are no longer questioned, but that, upon further investigation, are seen to be questionable.[22] The best way to bring these opinions to light and to subject them to the critical scrutiny necessary for us to appreciate how they condition the debate over music's social significance is to turn to those writers of the past whose thinking is not governed by the unquestioned conventions of thought that prevail in our own time and place.

2

Plato's Music of the Soul

PLATO IS ONE OF THE MOST CELEBRATED PHILOSOPHERS of the Western tradition, and the *Republic* is widely regarded as his greatest work. Therefore, it is not surprising that a number of elements of the *Republic* are familiar to most educated people. It is well known, for example, that the *Republic* is a dialogue depicting a conversation between Socrates, Plato's teacher and the first political philosopher, and a number of young men, the most active participants among them being Glaucon and Adeimantus, Plato's brothers. It is also well known that the conversation's aim is to discover the nature of justice and whether the just life is superior to the unjust, and that the participants investigate these matters by founding a "city in speech," a theoretical city that will manifest perfect justice. This discussion leads Socrates to propound a number of ideas famously associated with the *Republic*. Some of those notions are political (such as communism of property, the abolition of the private family, sexual equality, and the rule of philosopher-kings), some are psychological (such as the contention that the human soul is made up of three distinct parts), and some are metaphysical (such as the belief in ideas or forms that transcend the material world and are the source of all intelligibility and being).

23

Less familiar—though not less important—is Socrates' account of the political, psychological, and even metaphysical significance of music and his attribution of this significance not only, or even primarily, to the words of songs, but to music itself—to musical rhythm and harmony. In Book III of the *Republic* Socrates claims that music education is "most sovereign" because of rhythm and harmony's power "vigorously [to] lay hold of" the "soul."[1] Belief in this power is the point of departure for all the musical political philosophers, and from which the participants in our current debate, in their preoccupation with lyrics, can learn.

Socrates indicates that by means of this power the proper rearing in rhythm and harmony contributes considerably to the well-being of the individual and the political community by fostering in the soul an attraction to order that leads first to moderation, which makes possible an orderly and virtuous politics, and ultimately to philosophy, the activity in which the soul finds its most complete fulfillment.

The Beautiful Music of the Beautiful City

Socrates offers his account of music in the larger context of a discussion of the education of the guardian class of the city in speech, the class of citizens that will fight for the city in war and enforce the law at home.[2] This education, which consists of "gymnastic for bodies and music for the soul," comes to light as the solution to a political problem. The guardians are warriors and therefore must possess the quality known as spiritedness, which makes the soul "fearless and invincible in the face of everything."[3] It seems, however, that if they are not to be savage to each other and to the other citizens, they must also possess the opposite quality of gentleness. Socrates and his companions are faced with a dilemma: how to combine these two opposed qualities in the same human being.

The problem seems insoluble, and the good guardian impossible, until Socrates remembers that these two qualities are in fact successfully combined in noble dogs, who are gentle with those they know and savage with those they do not know. Such dogs are, Socrates argues somewhat playfully, philosophic in the sense that they define what is their own and what is alien by knowledge and ignorance. Similarly, the good guardian who combines gentleness for his own with savageness for strangers will have to "be a philosopher and a lover of learning."[4] This early association of the guardian class with philosophy prepares Socrates' later argument that rearing in rhythm and harmony, which is later identified as the most important part of the guardians' education, is capable of inclining one toward the philosophic life.

Socrates begins the main body of his account by defining music broadly as including both "speeches and tales" as well as "song and melody." Melody, he says, is composed of the elements of "speech, harmonic mode, and rhythm." For the rules governing the element of speech, Socrates refers his companions back to their earlier discussion of the proper content and style of "speech that isn't sung," the considerations on poetry and tales. There the interlocutors had agreed that the political health of the city requires that the literary depiction of gods and heroic men be such that it fosters in the guardians courage, honesty, freedom from greed, and moderation, in the dual sense of submitting to the rule of the political authorities and of ruling in oneself the bodily appetites for food, drink, and sex.

Socrates next asserts that rhythm and harmony themselves, apart from any words they may accompany, relate to virtue and vice. Harmonic mode and rhythm, he says, "must follow the speech." That is, the harmony and rhythm of a melody must somehow be appropriate to the lyrics of the song. And since the poetry of the just city will only imitate the speech of good men when they act "steadily and prudently," Socrates attempts to discover which harmonic modes and rhythms correspond to which virtues and vices.

For the Greeks "harmony," which in the Greek is simply *harmonia*, referred not to what we think of as harmony: notes sounding

simultaneously to produce a chord. Harmony in this sense was almost unknown in ancient Greek musical practice. Instead, the term
signifies a series of pitches from which tunes are created, or, simply
put, what we would call a scale.[5] Socrates' use of *rhythmos*, on the
other hand, corresponds more closely to our understanding of
rhythm. It refers to the "meter and the accentuation of music following upon it."[6]

Socrates begins with harmony and, as he claims not to know the
modes, relies on Glaucon's technical knowledge of music to help identify which modes go with which character traits. Together they pro-
ceed to purge from the city in speech those modes inappropriate to
the qualities desirable in guardians. As wailing and lamenting in tales
and poetry have been excluded, there will be no need for wailing and
lamenting harmonic modes. Glaucon identifies these as the "mixed"
and "tight" Lydian modes and some similar ones. Further, Socrates
argues, those modes appropriate to symposia, with their accompanying "drunkenness, softness, and idleness," qualities unseemly for
guardians, must be banished. These would be, according to Glaucon,
some Ionian and the "slack" Lydian modes.

Rather than continue in this manner and list all of the modes that
will be disallowed—which presumably would be numerous, as
Socrates insists that "the things that are good for us are far fewer than
those that are bad"[7]—Socrates instead simply tells Glaucon which
modes should be left in the city: a "violent" mode and a "voluntary"
mode, the former to foster courage in war and the latter to encourage reasonableness in peace.[8] These, Glaucon responds, would be the
Dorian and Phrygian modes, respectively. The possibility of a "voluntary" harmonic mode, which Socrates associates with "persuading,"
prepares the way for a later argument about the connection between
reason and music.

These limitations on harmony imply further restrictions on certain musical instruments. As only two modes will be used in the city's
music, there will be no need, Socrates says, for "panharmonic" instru-

ments, those capable of playing a variety of modes. The lute and the harp will have to be banished, for they are able to sound many pitches and play many modes by virtue of being "many-stringed."[9] Socrates also proposes to eliminate the *aulos*, a reed instrument similar to the modern oboe, which he says figuratively is "the most many-stringed" instrument of all.[10] The *aulos*, though a wind instrument, is many-stringed in the sense that it is capable of producing many different pitches and therefore, like the lute and harp, is "panharmonic" and unfit for the just city. Only the lyre and cither are left as musical instruments "useful for the city." These had only seven strings, which would have limited the range of harmonic modes they could play.[11]

Socrates reminds his companions of the importance of this micromanagment of such apparent trivialities by recalling the presentation of these instruments in Greek myth. "It's nothing new we're doing," he says, "in choosing Apollo and Apollo's instruments ahead of Marsyas and his instruments." In the minds of the ancient Greeks, Apollo, the god of truth, whose "province was taken to be all that is serene, ordered, and rational," was associated with the lyre and the cither, constantly depicted with them in art and literature.[12] Marsyas —one of the satyrs, followers of Dionysus and creatures notorious "for their love of wine, women, and nymphs"[13]—was, on the other hand, connected with the *aulos*.[14] Now, it is plain that the things associated with the lyre and cither are more appropriate for guardians than those associated with the *aulos*. In choosing the music of Apollo over that of Marsyas, Socrates chooses for the guardians of the best city a way of life radically different from the rejected alternative. To use the terminology of Nietzsche, to which we will later return, Socrates chooses Apollinian culture over Dionysian.

Socrates then inquires about the kind of rhythms that will properly accompany the speeches which the guardians are to hear. Rhythms, like harmonic modes, must follow the speech of a good man. And as with harmonic modes, Socrates relies on Glaucon to tell which rhythms are appropriate for a good life. But this time Glaucon is at a loss. While he has technical knowledge of the various kinds of rhythms, he cannot say which "are imitations of which sort of life." Socrates, unable to remember with any precision what he has heard on the subject, says the matter will be turned over to Damon, his authority on music and its effect on the soul.[15]

Socrates goes on to argue that the rearing in music is "most sovereign" by arguing that there is a mutual influence of the appearance of things and the disposition of the soul. "Grace"—*euschemosune*, gracefulness or elegance or beauty of outward appearance—is both a visible manifestation of a good disposition of soul and an inducement to such a disposition.[16] Grace accompanies proper rhythm and harmony, which follow good style of speech, which in turn follows from a rightly ordered soul. Conversely, gracelessness follows from a lack of rhythm and harmony, which follow from bad style of speech, which in turn follow from a bad disposition.

Moreover, he contends, the outward appearance of things affects the soul. Therefore, it is crucial that young guardians be exposed only to those things that have a fine appearance, that have grace. Grace and gracelessness, moreover, can be found in much of the visible realm: in bodies and in all things that grow and even in the various products of all the arts, including not only painting but also more practical and mundane crafts like housebuilding. Hence Socrates' fear that the young, through "cropping and grazing" on products of the arts that have a "licentious, illiberal, and graceless" appearance, will "unawares put together one big bad thing in their soul." In contrast, surrounded by graceful images "something of the fine works will strike their vision and hearing" and will "with the fair speech lead them to likeness and friendship as well as accord." Thus Socrates contends that the city must supervise not only the poets, as he had argued earlier, but all craftsmen to prevent them from impressing a graceless appearance on their works. In this light it is not surprising that Socrates refers to the city in speech he and his companions are founding as the *kallipolis*, the "beautiful city," for the city's physical appearance itself is meant to be an education in beauty that elevates the souls of the young and draws them toward beauty of character.

It is in the context of his concern with the ability of appearances to shape the soul that Socrates makes his startling claim that "rearing in music is most sovereign." Of all the images, he contends, music has the most power, through its own grace or gracelessness, to encourage a good or bad disposition in the soul. It is crucial to note that Socrates attributes this power primarily to music itself and not to lyrics. It is rhythm and harmony, not words, that "most of all insinuate themselves into the inmost part of the soul and most vigorously lay hold of it in bringing grace with them; and they make a man most graceful if he is correctly reared, if not, the opposite." Proper rearing in rhythm and harmony fosters in a young human being "the right kind of dislikes," teaching him to "praise the fine things" and to "blame and hate the ugly."

This ability of rhythm and harmony to influence character so powerfully is partly attributable to their ability to speak to the soul at its earliest stages of development. Rhythm and harmony, Socrates argues, begin to shape a person's soul "before he is able to grasp reasonable speech." Moreover, "the beginning is the most important part of every work" because at that stage the thing being shaped is "most plastic" and thus most readily "assimilates itself to the model whose stamp anyone wishes to give to it."[17] Thus rhythm and harmony are a more important element of music education even than the tales told to young children, since the former begin to form their souls before they can understand the latter.

Simple Music

Elsewhere in the *Republic* Socrates suggests that the gracefulness encouraged by the guardians' rearing is characterized chiefly by the virtue of moderation, understood as control over bodily desires, and that this virtue is the product of music's simplicity. "Melodies and songs written in the panharmonic mode and with all rhythms," he contends, lead to "licentiousness," while "simplicity in music" gives rise to "moderation in souls." One who cannot be bewitched by "terrors" and "pleasures"—that is, one who can control his bodily desires—proves himself "to possess rhythm and harmony."

This concern with fostering moderation through simplicity of music can also be discerned in Socrates' initial discussion of the rhythm and harmony appropriate to the just city. He rejects "subtle" rhythms in favor of those "of an orderly and courageous life." Similarly, when he describes the desired effects of the city's "violent" mode he indicates that he does not want the guardians to display a courage characterized by passionate rage but instead by a calm and reflective valor. He therefore asks for a musical mode that will "appropriately imitate the sounds and accents of a man" who, in battle, "stands up firmly and patiently against chance." He similarly indicates that the city's "voluntary" mode, appropriate to the performance of a "peaceful deed," should imitate a man "holding himself in check . . . acting moderately and in measure and being content with the consequences."

Socrates suggests three ways in which simple music might foster moderation. First, simple rhythms and harmonies can calm the passions and create a taste for that calmness in the soul. Rhythm and harmony possess "by nature" a kind of "charm," as Socrates says in Book x, that allows them, as he says in Book III, to forcefully "lay hold of" the soul, bringing into it their own grace or gracelessness.[18] Or, as it is stated more directly in the Laws, "the imitation in songs" can "make the soul feel passions."[19] Rhythm and harmony thus appear to be a form of imitation in which one actively participates merely by hearing music. And Socrates warns that the active imitation of a disposition can, especially if "practiced continually from youth onwards," lead one to develop a taste for the actual "being" of that disposition. It seems, then, that the young, impressionable soul can be habituated in a lasting taste for moderation through its early exposure to the simple rhythm and harmony that are an image of moderation.

Second, simple music cultivates a lasting love of order that is necessarily accompanied by an aversion to the disorderliness of immoderation. Such music presents to the soul a kind of grace, an orderly simplicity. This can be seen if we reflect that a harmonic mode is itself a kind of order that can be perceived by the soul. A mode or scale, after all, is not a mere jumble of unrelated pitches but an ordered structure, a hierarchical arrangement of notes.[20] More than merely presenting the soul with a kind of order, however, simple rhythm and harmony also habituate the soul in a love for that order and for orderliness in general. This they do, again, by means of that charm they naturally possess and by which they so powerfully lay hold of the young and tender soul. Thus the impressionable pre-rational soul is, by means of a simple rhythm and harmony, habituated to find pleasure in the beauty of orderliness.

This love of order fostered by simple music in turn translates into an inclination toward moderation because moderate behavior is orderly and immoderate behavior disorderly. The immoderate man lives entirely at the whim of his passions and therefore cannot organize his activities according to a rational, coherent design. Socrates suggests this in his powerful description of the democratic man who lives according to pleasure and rejects moderation. His activities, Socrates suggests, are governed entirely by chance. Refusing to recognize any hierarchical ordering of the pleasures, "he hands over the rule within himself" to "whichever one happens along, as though it were chosen by the lot," "until it is satisfied; and then again to another, dishonoring none but fostering them all on the basis of equality." The democratic man "lives along day by day, gratifying the desire that occurs to him, at one time drinking and listening to the flute, at another downing water and reducing; now practicing gymnastic, and again idling and neglecting everything; and sometimes spending his time as though he were occupied with philosophy. Often he engages in politics and, jumping up, says and does whatever chances to come to him; and if he ever admires any soldiers, he turns in that direc-

tion; and if it's money-makers, in that one. And there is neither order nor necessity in his life, but calling this life sweet, free, and blessed
he follows it throughout."[21] By creating in the young soul a love for
order, music characterized by simplicity of rhythm and harmony
cultivates a kind of aesthetic distaste for precisely the irregularity of
behavior displayed by the immoderate man and an aesthetic attraction to the orderly behavior displayed by the moderate man.

The complexity of the panharmonic music Socrates condemns,
on the other hand, is dangerous to the young because it fosters a very
different disposition. It does not present such an unequivocal orderliness. On the contrary, it presents to the pre-rational soul an aural
experience at least bordering on chaos. Yet it still possesses the charm
that by nature accompanies meter, rhythm, and harmony. The result
is an ethically disastrous fostering in the young of a taste for disor-
der, or at least an absence of an aversion to the irregularity of immoderate behavior which—given the intensity of the pleasures of the
body—would amount to an inclination toward immoderation.

Third, after the soul has reached the stage at which it can grasp
reasonable speech, the persuasive power of rhythm and harmony can
be joined with noble speeches to further encourage virtue in the soul.
Socrates hints at this role for rhythm and harmony in Book x, where
he argues that the poetic man, even though he lacks understanding,
can use the power of music to make it seem as if he speaks very well
on any subject, even when he does not. Rhythm and harmony can
make a bad speech seem fair just as the bloom of youth can make an
ugly face seem attractive, Socrates says.[22] The charm of harmony and
rhythm, it stands to reason, could also be used in the opposite way,
to reinforce the fairness of speeches that really are fair. This is in fact
what Socrates accomplishes in Book iii, where he joins the graceful
harmonic modes and rhythms with the good style of speech of the
gentleman.

These observations, moreover, point to another aspect of the simplicity of good music. Understood here more broadly as poetry set

to rhythm and harmony, good music is simple in that it imitates only one way of life, a moderate and decent one, eschewing the complexity of music that indiscriminately imitates all manner of dispositions. The city's music is based upon the narrative style of the gentleman, which imitates only good men when they are acting rightly, while merely reporting, but not imitating, the actions of the vicious. It rejects the narrative style of the non-gentleman, which imitates all kinds of men in all kinds of activities, noble as well as base, virtuous as well as vicious. Only the actions and speeches of the good and moderate man should be set to rhythm and harmony. In the just city's music, moderation is encouraged by giving to moderate speeches alone the rhetorical support of rhythm and harmony.

Complex music would, on the other hand, foster the opposite disposition. It would present a variety of ways of life, or states of soul, without providing any sense that some are better or more to be desired than others. All are presented, and all are equally accompanied by the charm of rhythm and harmony. Thus the audience—and, again, particularly its young and impressionable members—is taught that all are equally desirable. Each type of character or activity is paraded onto the stage, and we are led by the sweetness of the music accompanying each one to approve it in its turn, never suspecting that some are more worthy than others. Given that, as Socrates says, the desires are by far the biggest and strongest part of the soul, an education that refuses to give special support to moderation is likely to lead directly to its opposite.

The Gentleman, the City, and the Order of the Soul

The central importance of the account of music to the *Republic*'s teaching can be seen if we reflect on how Socrates' education in rhythm and harmony moves in the direction of satisfying the demand made by Glaucon and Adeimantus in Book II, a demand in response to which the argument of the rest of the *Republic* is addressed. The brothers demand that Socrates offer the strongest possible defense of justice and provoke him with a powerful account of what they claim is the popular understanding of justice as something bad for the one who adheres to it. The many, they say, view justice as a kind of drudgery to be practiced only for the sake of its consequences. The two brothers insist that Socrates demonstrate that justice is choiceworthy in itself, apart from any external consequences, such as reputation or safety, that may follow from it. By marrying pleasure and virtue, the music education proposed by Socrates seems to satisfy this demand.

The man who receives a proper rearing in rhythm and harmony, Socrates claims, would have the "sharpest sense" for what isn't a fine product of art or nature. "And due to his having the right kind of dislikes, he would praise the fine things" and would "tak[e] pleasure in them and receiv[e] them into his soul." On the other hand, he will "blame and hate the ugly." Such a man would also be led by this rearing to take pleasure in a good disposition and the deeds that accompany it, and to find painful the opposite disposition and deeds. Indeed, the conversation between Socrates and Glaucon indicates that the beneficiary of the proper education in music will "most of all love" and "take delight in" those who have a good disposition of soul.[23]

In sum, Socrates says that the proper rearing in rhythm and harmony would cause one to "become a gentleman."[24] Such a man, moreover, finds vice in some way painful. In discussing the narrative style of the "real gentleman" Socrates suggests that he "can't stand forming himself according to, and fitting himself into, the models of worse men."[25] Such a man is willingly just and, unlike the many described by Glaucon, harbors no suppressed desire to behave unjustly.

Those who lack this musical education, however, are divided against themselves in a way the musically educated are not, and will secretly desire and take pleasure in injustice. In Book VIII Socrates says that the timocratic man, the lover of honor, will secretly love money and will "harvest pleasures stealthily, running away from the law like boys from a father." This outcome is a result of his having been educated not "by persuasion but by force," by neglect of music in favor of the training of the body. The oligarchic man, the lover of money, is in a similar position. He has many unruly desires within himself which he must hold down "forcibly": he restrains them by "necessity and fear, doing so because he trembles for his whole substance." He therefore is "more graceful than many" but, lacking the musical man's love for virtue's beauty, fails to practice "the true virtue of the single-minded and harmonized soul."[26]

Socrates insists on the political importance of his teaching on music. The guardians, he claims, "must beware of change to a strange form of music, taking it to be a danger to the whole. For never are the ways of music changed without the greatest political laws being moved."[27] To a modern reader the connection will likely be less than obvious. To an ancient writer such as Plato, however, music is politically important because of the crucial role it plays in fostering beauty or nobility of character, which the ancients generally take to be the purpose of political life. At the same time, Socrates suggests that even on a more modern understanding of the purpose of politics, one that stresses the mere maintenance of peace and public order, the proper rearing in music is no less important.

Even on this more modest account of the ends of politics it turns out that the immoderate, ungentlemanly disposition resulting from improper rearing in, or neglect of, rhythm and harmony is politically disastrous, while the moderate, gentlemanly disposition fostered by a proper rearing in them is politically salutary. Immoderation is hostile to civic peace because it leads to acts of injustice and thus to faction within the city. The city's decision to indulge the desires beyond what is necessary, Socrates argues in Book II, leads to "the unlimited acquisition of money," thus to the theft of the property of a neighboring city, and thus to war. Book IX's account of the unjust methods adopted by the tyrannical soul in the pursuit of unlimited gratification of desire makes clear that the same thing can happen among individuals within a city. Conflict is the inevitable result of having a community of such human beings, each seeking to gratify himself at the expense of the rest. Such citizens lead lives dedicated to feeding and copulating, and "for the sake of getting more of these things, they kick and butt with horns and hoofs of iron, killing each other because they are insatiable."[28]

Proper rearing in music, however, greatly diminishes the likelihood of such conflict and thus makes governing much easier, by producing citizens who are gentlemen—men who, because of their attraction to virtue, are able willingly to restrain their desires. A city with good music education will not have to bother with a multitude of laws designed to restrain conflict among citizens, laws regulating "contracts . . . libel, insult, lodging of legal complaints, and the appointment of judges . . . or anything else of the kind." Instead, the lawfulness the citizens receive from music will "accompany" them in everything, "setting right anything in the city that may have previously been neglected."[29]

Absent the moderate, gentlemanly disposition fostered by rhythm and harmony, however, the preservation of public peace is very difficult. Citizens who have not been trained in virtuous habits will, in order to contain the conflict arising from their injustices to each other, "spend their lives continually setting down . . . rules and correcting them, thinking they'll get ahold of what's best." They hope that lawmaking will, like some miracle drug, cure the illness of their city. But, trying to restrain by laws men who cannot restrain themselves is "like cutting off the heads of a Hydra." It is "useless and accomplishes nothing," other than "to make their illness more complicated and bigger."[30]

Socrates remarks that moderation involves ruling in oneself "the pleasures of drink, sex, and eating."[31] This virtue is also understood in a broader sense in the *Republic*. Ultimately it refers not merely to the governing of the passions but to the proper ordering of the whole soul. It means not merely the subordination of the desiring part of the soul but also a certain arrangement of all three elements: the rule of reason over spirit, the seat of anger, and the desires, associated with the pleasures of the body. Hence, a man is called "moderate" because of the "friendship and accord" of the three parts of his soul, "when the ruling part and the two ruled parts are of a single opinion that [reason] ought to rule and don't raise faction against it." Moderation in this sense "is like a kind of harmony"; it "stretches throughout the whole" soul, "from top to bottom of the entire scale," making each part "sing the same chant together," in agreement as to which should rule.[32]

Rhythm and harmony certainly contribute to moderation in this sense insofar as they tame the desiring part, which is said by Socrates to be "most of the soul in each man" and thus presumably the more likely of the two ruled parts to overpower reason and disrupt the order of the whole soul.[33] But if rhythm and harmony are fully to establish this moderation, they must also somehow tame the spiritedness, the element associated with anger and ambition, for it too can dominate the soul contrary to the order Socrates wishes to establish.

Socrates explicitly asserts that rhythm and harmony can calm the spirited element of the soul. His account of how they accomplish this suggests that it is intimately related to their ability to strengthen reason. A full explanation of this power, then, must come after we have seen how rhythm and harmony contribute to the philosophic life, the life of reason, and how that life fulfills the human soul's deepest longings.

The Music of the Mind

Socrates' discussion of music suggests that there is some connection between the correct rearing in rhythm and harmony and one's capacity for reason or philosophy. For example, Socrates claims that "when reasonable speech comes" the man who has been properly educated in music "would take most delight in it, recognizing it on account of its being akin." Similarly, in his discussion of gymnastic, Socrates says that the philosophic part of the soul is "awakened" and "trained" and has its "perceptions purified" through partaking in "speech" and "the rest of music." Here, by referring to speech and the "rest of music," Socrates suggests that rhythm and harmony alone, apart from speech, play a role in preparing the soul for philosophy. Conversely, one who neglects "music and philosophy" becomes a "misologist," a hater of reason, and "unmusical."

Whatever the relationship between music and reason, education in music is not simply equivalent to education in philosophy. This much is made clear in Book VII, where Socrates and Glaucon consider what kind of education has the power to lead a soul from the realm of mere becoming, the world evident to the senses, up to the contemplation of what truly is, the realm of the ideas or forms. Glaucon argues, and Socrates agrees, that the music education of Book III does not do this. It merely transmits to the guardians a "rhythmicalness" and "harmoniousness" of habits, but not knowledge. This rearing in music trains the soul in virtuous dispositions but does not teach it to rise to the contemplation of the unchanging truth, which is philosophy.

In what way, then, is reasonable speech "akin" to rhythm and harmony? Reflection on passages in the *Republic* suggests three ways rhythm and harmony might prepare the soul for philosophy.[34]

First, although music's formation of the character does not equal an education in philosophy, it is nonetheless true that the *Republic* teaches that the pursuit of philosophy requires a certain kind of character fostered by proper rearing in music. Of particular concern here is moderation with regard to bodily pleasures, for it seems to be both the particular virtue fostered by the *Republic*'s music and to be crucial to philosophy. Such a view is implied in Book VI, when Socrates says that those who will be philosophic rulers must "take very good care of their bodies at the time they are growing and blooming into manhood, thus securing a helper for philosophy." We are led by this passage to conclude that an unhealthy body is a hindrance to philosophy, and we suspect that it is because of the pain that it occasions, which would constantly torment the soul and distract it from philosophic activity. But an unhealthy, immoderate soul also experiences a pain that distracts it and leaves it incapable of philosophy. For the "desiring part" of the soul can, "by its joy or pain," "disturb the best part," reason, and thus impede its activity. But Socrates suggests in Book ix that the tyrannical man, the man who exercises no restraint over his desires, experiences this kind of pain almost without respite, for his desires are so intense, and therefore so difficult to satisfy, that he must constantly seek out more and more resources, lest his desires "cry out" and "sting" his soul and he be "caught in the grip of great travail and anguish."[35]

The relationship between moderation and philosophy is made most explicit in Book vii. There Socrates suggests that some men with intellectual capacity are vicious and that their disposition toward the pleasures of the body turns their vision away from the philosophic contemplation of the truth. If, he says, the vicious part of such a nature "were trimmed in earliest childhood and its ties of kinship with becoming were cut off—like leaden weights, which eating and such pleasures as well as their refinements naturally attach to the soul and turn its vision downward—if, I say, it were rid of them and turned toward the true things, this same part of the same human beings would also see them most sharply, just as it does those things toward which it is now turned."[36]

Second, Socrates suggests in Book vi that the proper education in music goes beyond merely quieting the lower desires that can impede philosophic activity and actually fosters a kind of inclination toward philosophy. He states that an "unmusical and graceless nature" is drawn toward lack of "measure," suggesting that the opposite is also true, that a musical and graceful nature is drawn toward measure. And since "truth is related to . . . measure," such a nature will be drawn toward truth and, therefore, toward philosophy: "let us seek for an understanding endowed by nature with measure and charm, one whose nature grows in such a way as to make it easily led to the idea of each thing that is."[37]

The simple, orderly rhythm and harmony of the city in speech, possessing the charm of all music, creates in young guardians a lasting inclination toward what is graceful and orderly and an aversion to what is graceless and chaotic. Yet philosophy contemplates the natural order of things. Socrates says in Book VI that the philosopher "sees and contemplates things that are set in a regular arrangement and are always in the same condition," things that "remain all in order according to reason." The philosopher, he continues, keeps company "with the divine and orderly."[38] Rhythm and harmony can provide an inclination toward the orderly and thus can incline the soul toward philosophy.[39]

Third, and finally, one wonders whether the proper education in rhythm and harmony can actually somehow increase one's aptitude for philosophic activity by increasing one's intellectual capacity. This may seem somewhat speculative, not to say implausible, but it is not unreasonable to think that the right kind of rhythm and harmony, by exercising the pre-rational soul's ability to perceive order, could increase its ability to engage in rational thought.

This possibility will be discussed later at some length. For now it is sufficient to observe that some contemporary research indicates that the same parts of the human brain may be at work in processing music, language, and spatial-temporal reasoning. On the basis of such evidence one might reasonably suspect that exposure to the right kind of music in childhood could provide a kind of mental exercise that would lead to a lasting enhancement of the mind's capacity for rational thought. Perhaps in this third way, too, "reasonable speech" is akin to rhythm and harmony.

Human Nature and Human Happiness

At this point it is even more clear that Socrates' rearing in rhythm and harmony goes far toward satisfying Glaucon and Adeimantus's demand that justice be shown to be beneficial to the individual who lives it. This education not only produces a gentleman, one whose attraction to order draws him toward the self-government of virtue in general and moderation in particular. Ultimately, it produces a philosopher, one whose attraction to order draws him to the contemplation of eternal truth, an activity he finds so engaging that he is uninterested in the goods for which men typically commit injustice and therefore does not find the restraint of justice unpleasant.

Finally, however, whether the rearing in rhythm and harmony truly satisfies the brothers' demand depends on whether the longing for order, and the accompanying moderation and inclination toward philosophy it fosters, are in conformity with human nature. On the view of human nature advanced by Glaucon and Adeimantus in Book II, they are not. Glaucon claims that "any nature naturally pursues as good" the "desire to get the better." By "getting the better" he apparently means the unlimited indulgence of the bodily desires. Hence his assertion that any man would, if given the power of invisibility, use that power to "take what he wanted from the market" and to "go into houses and have intercourse with whomever he wanted." This understanding of human nature is also implicitly endorsed by Adeimantus at the beginning of Book IV, when he charges that the strictness of the way of life Socrates is imposing on the guardians will not make them happy. According to this view, the attraction to order and the moderation and philosophy to which it leads are contrary to human nature. At the deepest level of the soul, they go against the grain. Socrates' musical education does not satisfy the brothers' demand. On the contrary, this disposition, no matter how pleasant it is made to appear by the charm of rhythm and harmony, is a distortion of human nature and therefore productive of unhappiness.[40]

But Socrates rejects this understanding of human nature and human happiness as "foolish" and "adolescent," and in a number of passages indicates that the quieting of the passions by simple rhythm and harmony is not merely an unnatural frustration of the soul's longings. He claims, for example, that a man is "better and happier" when the desires in him are ruled and "worse and more wretched" when they rule. Also, he argues in Book IV that the order of soul in which the desires and the spirit are subordinated to reason is "according to nature," that any other arrangement is "contrary to nature," and that therefore the former can be understood as a kind of health, and the latter a kind of sickness, of soul. Since health is naturally desirable, Glaucon admits that, on this understanding, justice, or moderation, or the proper ordering of the soul's parts, is in itself profitable.[41]

But why does Socrates believe this arrangement of the parts of the soul, produced by proper rearing in rhythm and harmony, is healthy? First, and most obviously, it seems healthy because the alternative arrangement, one in which the desires rule the soul, is characterized by pain—a sign of illness. The tyrannical man is pained in his soul because he has a "noisy crowd" of desires that "cry out" for satisfaction, and as a result his soul is full of "complaining, sighing, lamenting," and "suffering."[42] By calming these desires, the rearing in rhythm and harmony eases this pain and therefore establishes a healthy disposition of soul.

Ultimately, however, the proper rearing in rhythm and harmony is good for the individual soul not so much because it provides a kind of repose that is preferable to the painful agitation of uncontrolled desire but more because it makes possible, and leads the soul toward, the experience of a positive good—the fulfillment, the happiness, of the human soul as a whole.

Simple rhythm and harmony's inculcation of a taste for order produces a character that is capable of, and longs for, philosophic contemplation. But such an activity is the satisfaction of a natural desire of the soul. The lowest part of the soul, Socrates says, is called the "desiring" part as a kind of shorthand, because of the "intensity of the desires concerned with eating, drinking, sex, and all their followers." In fact, however, each of the parts of the soul has a desire and a pleasure proper to it. The rational part is, then, "entirely directed toward knowing the truth as it is"; it is "learning-loving and wisdom-loving."[43] The life of philosophy to which the rearing in rhythm and harmony leads provides the satisfaction of a natural human longing and thus conduces to our happiness.

There is, moreover, reason to believe that the satisfaction of this part of the soul constitutes human happiness entire. This is suggested, first of all, in Socrates' image of man proposed in Book IX. In that image the desiring part of the soul is represented by a many-headed beast, the spirited part by a lion, and the rational part by a human being, indicating that the reasoning part of the soul is the distinctly human part. We are led to suspect that the happiness of this part will be, more than any other happiness, human happiness itself.

Many other passages in the *Republic* support this view. For example, in his discussion of the idea of the good, knowledge of which is the end of philosophic investigation, Socrates says that "this is what every soul pursues and for the sake of which it does everything." Moreover, Socrates argues in Book X that an understanding of the soul "such as it is in truth" must look to "its love of wisdom," that "its true nature" is that "it is akin to the divine and immortal and what is always" and that it "longs to keep company" with them. Socrates' repeatedly asserts that the philosophic life is the happiest.[44]

We are now in a position to understand more fully how simple, graceful rhythm and harmony can cultivate in the soul a taste for order. The human soul is by nature akin to the divine things and longs to keep company with them. But these things are, as we have seen, orderly, and there is a kinship between the soul and the cosmic order. The soul is by its nature responsive to this order and longs for it. Rhythm and harmony's cultivation of this taste is not an unnatural distortion of the soul's nature nor even an artificial putting into

the soul of something that is not already there. It is rather like the
education in philosophy proper, a turning of the soul toward that
which it has the power and desire to see. This rearing provides the
young soul with its earliest, most immature, experience of the order
for which it naturally longs.

Moreover, there is a kinship between the order of simple music
and the cosmic order which is sought by philosophy. In Book x's poetic account of the cosmos, Socrates describes a set of eight revolv-
ing whorls. On the lip of each "is perched a Siren, accompanying its
revolution, uttering a single sound, one note; from all eight is produced the accord of a *single harmony.*" The cosmos, like Socrates'
music, is not, it seems, panharmonic. There is some real continuity
between the immature soul's charming experience of order in rhythm
and harmony and the mature soul's final experience of it in philosophic contemplation. And perhaps this is why Socrates characterizes the grasping of the intelligible things "the song itself that dialectic
performs."[45]

Music is of great political importance in the *Republic* because of
the contribution it makes to the flourishing of the city and of the
individual. A proper rearing in music, one which exposes the young
soul to the orderly beauty of a graceful and simple rhythm and harmony, calms the passions and produces the moderate character that
avoids the pain of the tyrannical soul and that is necessary to an orderly and virtuous politics. Moreover, it stimulates the soul's natural longing for intelligible order and fosters a disposition inclined to
philosophy, the activity which seeks to grasp the intelligible order of
the universe and in which human beings find full happiness. We turn
now to Aristotle's *Politics* to see how Plato's pupil develops these
themes.

❦ 3 ❦

Aristotle's Musical Education

ARISTOTLE IS KNOWN not only as Plato's pupil and friend but also as his critic. In Book 1 of the *Nicomachean Ethics*, Aristotle hesitates to criticize the theory of ideas because of his friendship for its author. Yet he proceeds anyway, observing that "it would seem to be obligatory, especially for a philosopher, to sacrifice even one's closest personal ties in defense of the truth."

With regard to the political implications of music, Aristotle found the tension between friendship and truth less pronounced, for his teaching on this issue is to a large extent in harmony with that of Plato's Socrates. Hence, we may speak generally of an ancient approach to the relationship of music and politics. Like Plato's Socrates, Aristotle indicates that music is of great political importance because of its role in the moral education of the young. Like Plato's Socrates, he argues that the right kind of music can inculcate moderation in the soul and thus foster the well-being of the political community and the individual. Such moderation contributes to the stability of even imperfect political regimes and prepares the soul for the happiness of moral virtue and ultimately for the even more complete happiness of the philosophic life. In order to explicate these issues further, then, we turn to Book 8 of the *Politics*, which, in the context of his account

45

of the best regime, contains Aristotle's reflections on the relationship of music to politics.[1]

The Primacy of Music Education

Aristotle begins Book 8 of the *Politics* by asserting the supreme political importance of the education of children. It "would be disputed by no one," he writes, that "the legislator must make the education of the young his object above all."[2] By the education of the young Aristotle does not mean, as a contemporary reader might suppose, merely the learning of information, but rather a "preparatory education and habituation" with a view to the "actions of virtue." Such actions are the principal business of politics. The city, Aristotle argues, has as its end "living well" or "noble actions."[3] But because virtue is "the product of habit," the central concern of the statesman must be education understood as habituation or character formation.[4] Aristotle, therefore, suggests that "the principal care" of "political science" is "to produce a certain character in the citizens, namely to make them virtuous, and capable of performing noble actions."[5]

Ultimately, the most powerful such habituation must be an especially central concern to the statesman, and this is the education of children. This training is of supreme importance, Aristotle holds with Plato, because the young are so impressionable. Hence, "everything mean" should "be made foreign to the young," because "we are fonder of the first things [we encounter]."[6]

To say that the education of children is of supreme political importance, moreover, is to say that it is of supreme importance simply, because for Aristotle the end of politics is the final end of human life itself: happiness, that supreme good which is self-sufficient and choiceworthy for its own sake. This Aristotle finds in the distinctive function of man, which is not mere living, which we share with plants, nor the life of physical sensation, which we share with animals, but rather the activity of the uniquely human "rational part" of the soul "in conformity with excellence or virtue."[7] Education of the young, then, is of supreme human importance because it contributes decisively to our ability for virtuous action, which is the end of human life, in which human beings find their final and complete happiness.

The political importance Aristotle gives to childhood education explicitly, he gives in the rest of Book 8 implicitly to the education of children in music specifically. For music education alone among the disciplines discussed turns out to be "education" in the sense of formation of character with a view to virtue. In Chapter 3 Aristotle introduces four things in which children are typically educated: letters, drawing, gymnastics, and music. Of these, the first two are undertaken not with a view to what is noble but rather what is practical or useful. Specifically, letters are useful with a view to "business, management of the household, learning, and many political activities," and drawing "with a view to judging more finely the works of artisans." Aristotle argues, however, that "training in things useful for life" should be brought into childhood education only to the extent that it does not make the pupil vulgar, that is, to the extent that it does not render "the body, soul, or mind of free persons useless with a view to the practices and actions of virtue." Education in the useful things has little or nothing positive to contribute to virtue.

Gymnastic education is more ambiguous. Aristotle does observe at the beginning of Chapter 3 that gymnastic is customarily practiced "as contributing to courage," which is a moral virtue. But he is not advancing his own teaching so much as describing common practice. Indeed, in passages in which Aristotle speaks for himself, gymnastic appears unrelated to preparing one for virtuous action. For example, in his discussion of the use of music by the earliest Greek educators, he claims that gymnastic is useful "with a view to health and vigor," and later he remarks that children ought to be trained in it because "it makes the disposition of the body of a certain quality."[8]

Only education in music, then, remains to prepare the soul for virtuous activity. Aristotle argues explicitly that music has this power.

Music "contributes something to virtue" and therefore "the young must be educated in it," he says, because it is "evident through many things" that "we become of a certain quality in our characters on account of it." Here it is important to note that this claim is advanced by Aristotle, as by Plato, on behalf not of music understood as poetry and stories, and not even of music understood as songs or poetry set to tunes, but rather on behalf of music understood as melodies apart from lyrics. Aristotle points to the "tunes of Olympus," which all agree induce "inspiration," a "passion of the character connected with the soul." Now, the "tunes" to which Aristotle refers are tunes in the strict sense, for the Greek *melos* signifies a melody derived from a particular mode, not a song with lyrics. Indeed, the tunes of Olympus were not vocalized at all. Rather, they were instrumentals, solo pieces for the flute or *aulos*, apparently in the Phrygian mode.[9] This focus on music as the character-forming element in education is made even more explicit later when Aristotle states that "we see that music depends on tune composition and rhythms" and that, therefore, "we should not overlook the power that each of these has with a view to education."[10]

Rhythm and harmony, Aristotle contends, can imitate or represent various states of character, impress them upon the soul of the listener, and induce in him a kind of pleasure at being in such states of character. And in light of our tendency to love the first things we encounter, this power of music, when practiced upon the young, can create in them a lasting inclination toward the states of character represented.

In his *Poetics*, Aristotle repeatedly asserts the capacity of harmony and rhythm to imitate various states of character.[11] There he claims that "good" and "inferior" men are the objects of artistic imitation and that artists represent them in "rhythm and speech and harmony, using these means either separately or in combination." "Flute-playing and harp-playing," he continues, employ "harmony and rhythm alone," and because of the imitative power of these things the "diversities" of character "may certainly be found" in these arts.[12]

Harmony and rhythm, furthermore, impress upon the listener the states they imitate. Aristotle writes in Book 8 of the *Politics* that "all who listen to imitations come to experience similar passions." He continues, observing that "in rhythms and tunes there are likenesses particularly close to the genuine natures of anger and gentleness, and further of courage and moderation and of all the things opposite to these and of the other things pertaining to character," and that "we are altered in soul when we listen to such things."[13] In relation to some harmonies, such as the Mixed-Lydian, listeners are in a state of "grief and apprehension." Others, the relaxed harmonies, render men "softer of mind." Alone among the harmonies, Dorian induces "a middling and settled state." Last, Phrygian makes them "inspired." Apparently, rhythms possess the same power to impress a state of character on the soul of the listener: "some of them have a character that is more steadfast, others a character marked by movement, and of these some have movements of a cruder, others of a more liberal sort."

In addition, Aristotle claims that music "involves a natural pleasure" and thus that "the practice of it is agreeable to all ages and characters." But if rhythm and harmony can present to and impress upon the soul good states of character, and accompany those states of soul with a certain natural pleasure, and if this is done to the souls of the young, which are so impressionable, then it would seem that music education can cultivate a lasting attraction to virtue and aversion to vice, that it can produce a character for whom virtuous activity is pleasant.

This is, indeed, what Aristotle suggests in Chapter 5 of Book 8. After reminding us that music belongs among "the pleasant things," he notes that "virtue is connected with enjoying in correct fashion" and goes on to suggest that it is therefore possible by means of music to "become habituated to . . . judging in correct fashion of, and enjoying, respectable characters and noble actions" and to feel "hatred" for their opposites. Strictly speaking, of course, music can only dispose us to feel affection for the harmonic and rhythmic imitations of virtue. But, Aristotle argues, this amounts to the same thing. "Habituation to feel pain and enjoyment in similar things," he writes, "is close to being in the same condition relative to the truth," for "if someone enjoys looking at the image of something for no other reason than" its form, "then the very study of the thing" itself "must necessarily be pleasant" to him. Thus, love of noble tunes translates into love of nobility.

Aristotle's concern with music, like Plato's, elaborates his more general concern with the influence of "graceful" and "graceless" images. Just as Plato's Socrates contends that all images can influence the disposition for good or ill, but rhythm and harmony most of all because of their unmatched power to lay hold of the inmost part of the soul, so Aristotle claims that the "likeness of characters" is "in visible things present only to a slight degree" in comparison to its presence in "rhythms and tunes." In agreement with his teacher that the young soul is extremely malleable, Aristotle shares his concern that even the less potent influence of visible images be used to foster a good disposition. Hence he argues that, for the sake of the young, the city must contain "no statue or painting" that is an "imitation" of "unseemly" actions and that the young should not study the paintings of Pauson, who depicted men as worse than they are, but rather those of Polygnotus, who "depicted men as better than they are."[14] Hence, also, Aristotle's concern that even private homes and the city's walls should be designed not only with a view to "military requirements" but also with a view to "ordered beauty."[15] His attention to these details indicates that he shares Socrates' concern that the young be "benefitted by everything" and that the beneficial influence of such "fine works" will begin to lead them to beauty of soul.[16]

Moderation and Moral Virtue

Later passages in Book 8 suggest that Aristotle's music education, like Socrates', aims in particular at cultivating a kind of moderation, understood as a general calmness of the passions. "With a view to education," Aristotle contends, one should use those tunes and harmonies "that relate to character," and he specifies that "Dorian is of this sort." Now, Dorian music has already been identified in the *Politics* with a kind of moderation. In his earlier discussion of the state of soul communicated by each of the harmonies, Aristotle writes that Dorian "above all" the others is able to put us "in a middling and settled state." He suggests that it is precisely this moderate quality that makes Dorian music so appropriate to the education of the young. He observes that "we praise the middle between extremes and assert it ought to be pursued," and "since Dorian has this nature relative to the other harmonies, it is evident that it is appropriate for younger persons to be educated in Dorian tunes." Conversely, Aristotle also condemns the educational use of the kind of music that fosters an extreme agitation of the passions. "The Socrates of the *Republic*" is wrong, he says, to make use of the Phrygian mode, because it is "characteristically frenzied and passionate."[17]

Aristotle's education thus turns out to be primarily the cultivation, by means of the imitative power and natural pleasure of the Dorian mode, of a character that can find pleasure in a settled state of soul, a middling state of passion. Aristotle's music aims, like that of the *Republic*, to foster moderation. Yet moderation is only one of many ethical virtues for Aristotle. How, then, are we to understand Aristotle's earlier suggestion that music education prepares the soul for virtue itself and his statement here that good character generally is somehow related to the moderating effects of the Dorian mode?

Certainly Aristotle's account of moral virtue in the *Ethics* suggests some similarity between this middling or settled state and the life of moral virtue generally. There it is said that "moral qualities are so

constituted as to be destroyed by excess and deficiency . . . and preserved by the observance of the mean" and that moral virtue involves
the finding of a "middle state."[18] Similarly, Book 4 of the *Politics* refers to the *Ethics* as having established that "virtue is a mean" and that
therefore "the middling sort of life is best."[19]

Aristotle's account also makes clear, however, that there is a distinct difference between this settled state of passion and the true activity of moral virtue. Although the role played by pleasures and
pains in corrupting men may lead some to "define the virtues as states
of impassivity or tranquility," these thinkers err insofar as they use
these terms "absolutely, without adding 'in the right or wrong manner' and 'at the right or wrong time' and the other qualifications." The
"mark of virtue" is to feel the mean amount of passion, but this is not
to be in a continually impassive state, rather to feel the passions as
reason dictates: "at the right time, on the right occasion, toward the
right people, for the right purpose and in the right manner."[20]

This difference between the state of soul fostered by Aristotle's
music education and the actual activity of moral virtue can be ex-
plained by recalling that Aristotle, despite the great importance he
attributes to the character formation of the young, claims only a limited power for it. It provides, he says, a "*preparatory* education and
habituation" with a view to "the actions of virtue" but not an education in the actions themselves.[21] Indeed, Aristotle insists that we become just, temperate, and brave not by exposure to decent music but
by actually performing just, temperate, and brave acts.[22] Music education is therefore related to the whole of virtue, not in the sense that
it makes one virtuous, but rather in the sense that it makes it easier
to become virtuous.

This settled state of soul cultivated by Dorian tunes prepares one
for the activity of virtue because one's capacity for moral reasoning
is disrupted by passion. Aristotle observes that "he that lives at the
dictates of passion" cannot be deterred from vicious action by "theory
and teaching," since he "will not hear or understand the reasoning of

one who tries to dissuade him."[23] More specifically, Aristotle argues that living well requires the performance of two intellectual tasks: "correct positing of the aim and end of actions" and "discovering the actions that bear on the end."[24] That is to say, virtuous activity requires prudence, the twofold ability to discern the first principles of conduct, the moral virtues, and to discover by "calculation" how, in variable circumstances, these virtues can be realized by means of particular actions.[25]

With regard to the former capacity Aristotle notes that the Greek term for "temperance" or moderation literally "signifies 'preserving prudence.'" This is so, he argues, because temperance "does in fact preserve our belief as to our own good," since pleasure and pain tend to destroy or pervert our beliefs concerning action: "The first principles of action are the end to which our actions are means; but a man corrupted by love of pleasure or fear of pain, entirely fails to discern any first principle, and cannot see that he ought to choose and do everything as a means to this end."[26]

Aristotle indicates that the latter capacity is likewise impeded by passion. In the *Ethics* he contends that there are those who apprehend the first principles of virtuous conduct but are nevertheless unable to apply them to their particular circumstances because when under the influence of passion they, in a sense, forget those principles, like men who are asleep, mad, or drunk.[27]

If our intellectual capacities are impaired by excessive passion, however, they are preserved by calmness of the passions and therefore are more readily exercised by those who possess the type of character fostered by Aristotle's Dorian music. It is for this reason that Aristotle says that a proper education in music makes one able to judge not merely noble tunes but noble things themselves.

Again, the settled state of passions fostered by Dorian music is not itself virtuous, for virtue involves not a persistent mediocrity of the passions but rather the directing of the passions by reason. Nevertheless, for the passions to be directed by reason they must first be calmed by music, and so Aristotle's habituation in tranquility by means of rhythm and harmony is necessary if we are to experience that happiness that accompanies morally virtuous activity.

Aristotle also teaches that virtue requires something beyond the ability to see the end and discern the means. To be virtuous in the full sense, one must enjoy virtuous activity. The "man who does not enjoy doing noble actions is not a good man at all: no one would call a man just if he did not like acting justly, nor liberal if he did not like doing liberal things, and similarly with the other virtues." One might think that on Aristotle's teaching there is no difficulty involved in enjoying virtuous actions. After all, he asserts that the life of active virtue is pleasant in itself and that the good man "has no need of pleasure as a sort of ornamental appendage." Nevertheless, Aristotle also contends that this natural pleasure can only be experienced by those who have been correctly habituated. Habit can render some things pleasant that are not "naturally pleasant," and thus vicious activities that are not "actually pleasant" may become so "to ill-conditioned people." As a result, only a good man can be relied upon to judge correctly regarding what is truly pleasant according to nature.[28]

Aristotle suggests that by means of the pleasure induced by music one can be habituated not only to "judging in correct fashion" but also to "enjoying respectable characters and noble actions." Now that we have seen that Aristotle's primary aim is to use music to calm the passions, we can better appreciate how it contributes to the ability to enjoy virtue.

Pain occasioned by virtuous activity can obscure the natural pleasure of that activity. Aristotle writes that although the activity of the virtue of courage is really pleasant, "its pleasantness is obscured by the attendant circumstances," such as the suffering of wounds and death. But those whose passions are extreme experience constant pain and therefore cannot enjoy virtuous activity. The "profligate" man "desires all pleasures, or those that are most pleasant, and is led by his desire to pursue them in preference to everything else. He consequently feels pain not only when he fails to get them, but also from his desire for them, since desire is accompanied by pain; paradoxical though it seems that pain should be caused by pleasure."[29] Those who have excessive passions cannot take pleasure in virtue, because they desire constant gratification and are in pain when that gratification is denied, as it must be if their pleasures were to be governed by reason. Aristotle's education in Dorian music, by fostering a calmness of the passions, makes it possible to enjoy virtue.

In this light we can see how music extricates Aristotle from a dilemma. Virtue, as we have seen, requires habituation from childhood. But "children, like profligates, live at the prompting of desire" and therefore must be pained by the control of the passions that virtue requries.[30] The aim of their moral education is to teach them to enjoy virtue, but how can they be taught to enjoy what is painful?

The answer is found in Aristotle's observation that the use of music in the character formation of the young "is fitting in relation to the nature of those of such an age, for on account of their age the young do not voluntarily put up with anything that is not sweetened, but music by nature belongs among the sweetened things." The charm that accompanies rhythm and harmony, it seems, renders the subordination of the passions palatable to the young and thus enables them to endure the habituation that will enable them later to experience the natural pleasure of virtuous action.

Music and Contemplation

In Aristotle's teaching, as in Plato's, the most complete happiness is found in the life of philosophy. Aristotle argues that the highest happiness is ultimately realized in "activity in accordance with the highest virtue" and that this is "the virtue of the best part of us": our intellect.[31] Moreover, and again like Plato, Aristotle sees a connection between his education in music and the pursuit of philosophy.[32]

This connection is suggested by Aristotle's linking of music education with leisure, which is in turn associated with philosophy. Philosophic activity is the most leisured, Aristotle claims in the *Ethics*, because, like leisure, contemplation of the truth is desired for its own sake, aiming at no end beyond itself, while the "practical virtues," displayed in war and politics, are "unleisured" insofar as they aim at "securing something beyond" their own activity.[33] It may seem strange to the modern reader to link leisure, which is commonly thought to involve distraction from the serious by engaging in the frivolous, to the highest human activities. Aristotle was aware of this misapprehension because it was prevalent in his own day. Most men, he contends, mistake play, or rest from work, with serious leisure and hence with the end of human life. This error arises from a certain superficial similarity between the two. Just as play involves a pleasant rest from painful exertion, so serious leisure involves the natural and positive pleasure of enjoying the highest human good, philosophic contemplation. Also, just as the pleasure of serious leisure is not desired for the sake of any future good because it is complete in itself, so the pleasures of play are not "for the sake of anything that will be" but rather for the sake of things that "have been" in the past, "such as exertions and pain."

Music is often taken to be merely a kind of play. Nevertheless, Aristotle connects music not with counterfeit leisure but with contemplation: the leisure toward which music looks contains "the end of life for us," which is philosophy. He later remarks that "it is evident that there should be education" for leisure and then goes on to suggest that, of the four things in which the young are typically trained, only music can provide this education. Again, letters and drawing look to what is useful, and gymnastic is practiced with a view to the health of the body. Music, on the other hand, involves none of these things, and "what remains is that it is" studied "with a view to the pastime that is in leisure."

In Book 7 of the *Politics*, Aristotle argues that because "reason and intellect are the end of our nature . . . it is with a view to these that birth and the concern with habits should be handled."[34] As we have seen, music education is itself the habituation of the young that Aristotle has in mind, and thus it must be possible to handle it in such a way that it contributes to the life of reason and intellect. Moreover, Aristotle's argument that the flute or *aulos* ought to be kept out of education of the young because training in it "has nothing to do with the mind" also implies that music education can increase or diminish one's capacity for philosophy.

Aristotle's account of this power parallels that of the *Republic*. In the first place, philosophy appears to require that settled state the passions imparted by Dorian music. Aristotle contends that unlike moral virtue, which depends on habituation, "intellectual virtue is for the most part both produced and increased by instruction" or by "listening."[35] Listening well to this instruction, however, does not come naturally but in fact requires a preparatory habituation such as is provided by Aristotle's music. Hence, he suggests that only those instruments should be brought into education "that will make them good listeners either of music education or of the other [sort of education]."

Man is composed of both rational and passionate elements. And "whenever one of these two elements is active, its activity runs counter to the nature of the other."[36] Therefore, the intellectual activity of those who are accustomed to a ceaseless agitation of their passionate element will be impeded by that very agitation. Conversely, intellectual activity is facilitated in those whose passionate element has been habituated to a kind of quietness or tranquility. It is in this light that Aristotle remarks, in his discussion of the education of children, that learning "is accompanied by pain." And so it is to those who, like children, live by their feelings and thus must experience the sustained exercise of their reason as a painful impediment to that continual churning of the passions to which they are accustomed. Aristotle remarks elsewhere that "the philosopher has to arrive at some things by demonstration."[37] To be contemplated and enjoyed truths must first be discovered, and this requires long, patient, and rigorous thought. And those whose minds are distracted by the agitation of their passions, and the need to ease by gratification the pain that accompanies that agitation, are capable of this disciplined reasoning only with great difficulty, if they are capable of it at all.

Second, music can foster in the soul an inclination to take pleasure in, and thus to seek out, the rationally discernible order of nature. Music and nature are akin to the extent that both are characterized by a kind of orderliness. This kinship is indicated in Book 1 of the *Politics*, where Aristotle writes that "all of nature" is orderly in the sense that it is characterized by relationships of ruling and being ruled and that such order is found also in inanimate things, "for example in a harmony."[38] Thus music can, by the power of its natural pleasure exercised upon the impressionable souls of the young, create in them an enduring attraction to rationally discernible order and thus incline them towards philosophic investigation.

Finally, music to some extent can train the mind and develop its powers of reasoning. In Book 3 of the *Ethics* Aristotle argues that, although music involves hearing, and is thus one of the pleasures of the senses, the "lower animals" do not derive any pleasure from it.[39] He thus implies that it is a uniquely human pleasure that somehow engages the uniquely human faculty of reason.[40] In the *Poetics* he explicitly argues that the pleasure derived from music arises from the way in which it engages the reason. Men have from childhood, he argues, "an instinct for representation," and man differs from the other animals in that "he is far more imitative and learns his first lessons by imitating things." Thus, the pleasure involved in music is derived from a kind of learning. We enjoy seeing likenesses because "as we look, we learn and infer what each is," and learning "gives pleasure not only to philosophers but also in the same way to all other men, though they share this pleasure only to a small degree."[41] Moreover, Aristotle suggests that the kind of intellectual skills cultivated by listening to music are not unimportant. Later in the *Poetics* he writes that great skill in the use of metaphor "is the token of genius," for it "means an eye for resemblances."[42] But music, by presenting in harmony and rhythm imitations of the states of character, necessarily provides a kind of training in recognizing resemblances. Moreover, that the capacity to recognize resemblances is useful with a view to philosophic investigation is suggested by Aristotle's observation in the *Ethics* that "one is forced to explain," and thus to understand, "what is invisible by means of visible illustrations."[43]

Justice and Peace

Although Socrates' rearing in music is undertaken ultimately with a view to the highest and happiest way of life, it is at first proposed with a more mundane, though perhaps more pressing, concern in mind: the internal peace of the city. Socrates initially offers the rearing in rhythm and harmony as a way of keeping the citizens from being "savage" with one another, and the argument finally reveals that the calming of the desiring part of the soul effected by this education serves to prevent the factional conflict that must occur as a result of the injustices committed by those who have excessive desires to satisfy.

Aristotle's account reveals similar concerns. At the beginning of his treatment of education in Book 8 of the *Politics*, Aristotle indicates that the education of the young is of supreme political importance not only because it is necessary with a view to the aims of the best regime, moral and intellectual excellence, but also because it contributes to the preservation of even imperfect regimes. Where the legislator neglects education, he contends, "it hurts the regimes." "One should educate with a view to each sort" of regime, forming the character that is appropriate to and supportive of each, whether it is, for example, a democracy or an oligarchy.

Again, as education in music is the only character-forming education of the young presented by Aristotle, it must somehow help to preserve existing, imperfect regimes. It might seem that Aristotle's musical education in moderation is precisely what is not needed for such regimes. After all, that education looks toward the flourishing of moral and intellectual virtue and thus might be said to foster an aristocratic character. But Aristotle says that oligarchy is supported by an oligarchic character and democracy by a democratic character. Would it not, then, be more fitting to inculcate love of gain in the children of oligarchs and freedom, understood as living as one pleases, in the young of a democracy?

This apparent contradiction is resolved when we consider that the characters that support such regimes are not those given to the passions associated with them but instead those with the habits that tend to preserve them. Aristotle argues in Book 5 of the *Politics* that "to be educated relative to the regime is not to do the things that oligarchs or those who want democracy enjoy, but rather the things by which the former will be able to run an oligarchy and the latter to have a regime that is run democratically."[44] The lack of such an education is revealed in the fact that "in oligarchies the sons of the rulers live luxuriously" and in democracies the people wrongly understand freedom and consequently "everyone lives as he wants and 'toward whatever [end he happens] to crave.'"[45] This condemnation of luxury and living however one wants suggests that, whatever the differences between the spirits of oligarchy and democracy, there will be a need in both for moderation of the passions and hence for the music education Aristotle has outlined for his best regime.[46]

Even such commonplace regimes need moderation because immoderate desires lead to injustice, which in turn leads to factional conflict and the threat of revolution. Aristotle observes that "bodily gratifications" are "available in and through possessions."[47] The gratification of excessive desires requires a great many possessions. Now, such a superfluity of goods can only be come by in one of three ways: fortune, hard work, or injustice. The first cannot be relied upon, and the second defeats the purpose of those who seek after bodily pleasure. Injustice remains, and Aristotle suggests more than once that injustice results from excessive desire. In the *Ethics* he argues that immoderation often gives rise to prodigality, or looseness with money, which in turn involves not only excessive spending but also excessive getting of money: the prodigal are "mean" and "grasping." Desiring always to spend freely, but unable to do so because they soon exhaust their resources, they "are compelled to obtain supplies from others," and because of their indifference to "nobility of conduct, they are careless how they get their money, and take it from anywhere." That such people are driven by their desire not only to the unseemly but to the actually unjust is revealed when Aristotle claims that the prodigal tend to "follow degrading trades," such as brothel-keeping and loan-sharking, which involve taking "from wrong sources, and *more than their due*."[48] It is in this light that Aristotle comments elsewhere that the motives that lead men to commit injustice are depravity and incontinence and that we like "the self-controlled because they are not likely to commit injustice."[49]

That injustice arising from immoderation threatens to destroy regimes by provoking factional conflict is a central theme of Book 5 of the *Politics*. Aristotle reports that one of the "most evident" modes by which oligarchies "undergo revolution" is "when they treat the multitude unjustly," while they are made more lasting when "those occupying the offices treat well those outside the regime," particularly when they refrain from acting unjustly "toward the many with regard to profit."[50] Similarly, "democracies undergo revolution particularly on account of the wanton behavior of the popular leaders" who, currying favor with the people, seek to confiscate the goods of the well-off, thus causing them to combine and attempt the destruction of the regime.[51]

Political crises great enough to threaten the very existence of a regime, it seems, can arise from the excessive desires of the citizens. Aristotle's education of the young in Dorian music, then, contributes to the peace of cities and the preservation of regimes by producing citizens in whose souls the violent movements of the passions have been stilled.

The musical teachings of the *Republic* and the *Politics* are fundamentally in harmony. For both Plato's Socrates and Aristotle, a musical rearing in moderation assists the maintenance of public order by quieting the unruly passions that lead to injustice. For both, moreover, such an education also contributes to the higher aim of political life, the cultivation of human excellence, by preparing the soul for the activities of moral nobility and philosophic contemplation.

Before examining the very different understanding of how music contributes to human excellence offered by Rousseau and Nietzsche, we turn briefly to consider music's disappearance from political philosophy in the thought of the early moderns, whose lowering of the goal of political life rendered music politically irrelevant.

≈ 4 ≈

An Amusical Interlude

I T IS NOT MUCH OF AN EXAGGERATION to say that music, as an
issue of political consequence, vanishes in the political philosophy of early modernity. The intellectual architects of modern
liberalism do not acknowledge the public significance of music's
power over the soul. One seeks almost in vain for any recognition
of this issue in the works of Hobbes, Locke, and Montesquieu.

Such a search is only "almost" in vain because of the one excep-
tion to the early moderns' general tendency to ignore music.
Montesquieu, in *The Spirit of the Laws*, recognizes and agrees with
the ancient teaching on the political usefulness of the "power of music
over mores." Music, he contends, can arouse all the passions, and thus
"the ancients were right . . . when, under certain circumstances, they
preferred one mode of music to another for the sake of mores." The
classical republics needed something to mitigate the "harsh and savage" temper that their rigorous physical and military training tended
to produce. Thus they turned to forms of music that "can make the
soul feel softness, pity, tenderness, and sweet pleasure."[1]

Yet Montesquieu falls far short of endorsing Plato and Aristotle's
understanding of music's role in politics. He states that the ancients
were right in *certain circumstances* to use music for political purposes

63

and that this use is "one of the principles of *their* politics."[2] Nevertheless, the rest of *The Spirit of the Laws* suggests the undesirability of the political and moral circumstances that require music, indicating that the politics of the ancients, of which music is an important principle, is far removed from that of Montesquieu. This is made most clear in Montesquieu's account of the best form of government, which is far more commercial than martial and which omits any discussion of the political role of music.

The disappearance of music from political philosophy in the writings of the early moderns is, then, no mere fluke. On the contrary, it results from the rise of an understanding of how and toward what ends politics ought to be ordered very different from that advanced by the ancients. The ancients' interest in music arose from their larger concern with character formation, which they regarded as indispensably necessary to the end of politics, the fostering of moral and intellectual excellence. Character formation disappears in modern political teaching, however, because the early moderns rejected the idea that politics should or can aim at such lofty goals and advocated instead a politics oriented toward more mundane and achievable ends.

Modern thinkers such as Hobbes, Locke, and Montesquieu all reject the classical scheme as unrealistic.[3] They abandon as merely utopian a politics guided by the ancient account of a best regime, in which a musical education in moderation leads citizens to the happiness found in the activity of moral and intellectual virtue. In so doing they follow the lead of Machiavelli who, in *The Prince*, casts aside the classical understanding of the best regime as a guide to political action on the grounds that such a regime has never been established in practice. Machiavelli claims to depart "from the orders of others" insofar as he seeks to guide political action not on the basis of "imaginary . . . republics and principates that have never been seen or known to be in truth" but rather on the basis of the "effectual truth."

Unlike the ancients, he looks to "how one lives" rather than to "how one should live" as a basis for his political teaching.[4]

This effectual truth about how one lives in the real world, if not in the imaginings of Plato and Aristotle, is revealed by Machiavelli in Chapter III of *The Prince*: "It is a thing truly very natural and ordinary to desire to acquire; and when men who are able to do so do it, they are always praised or not blamed; but when they are not able and yet want to do so in every mode, here is the error and the blame."[5] The dominant part of human nature, that which drives the actions of most men most of the time, is selfish desire or passion.

The role of reason, then, is not to identify standards of human excellence in the pursuit of which the desires must be restrained. On the contrary, praise and blame—and by extension, as Machiavelli makes clear throughout *The Prince*, virtue and vice—are to be understood in relation to acquisition and the satisfaction of desire: virtue is associated with the ability to acquire and vice with the inability. Reason, in Machiavelli's account of human nature, has no higher end than to aid acquisition. Hence, his rejection of the political teaching of the ancients is based upon his conviction that their psychology is defective, that their account of the soul is no less imaginary than their account of the city. The ancients take as their political standard the possibility that, through the proper rearing in music, the passions can be calmed and hence the rest of the soul freed to find its truly natural happiness in moral virtue and, ultimately, philosophy. For Machiavelli this is simply impossible—or perhaps possible in so few people as to be politically irrelevant, effectually untrue. Put another way, Machiavelli casts his lot with the view articulated by Glaucon in Book II of the *Republic* that "the desire to get the better . . . is what any nature naturally pursues as good," in light of which Socrates' moderating music education must be regarded as contrary to nature and productive of unhappiness.[6]

Hobbes

This belief in the necessary subjection of reason to passion was adopted, and stated more explicitly, by Thomas Hobbes. Hobbes's now famous formulation states that "the Thoughts, are to the Desires, as Scouts, and Spies, to range abroad, and find the way to the things Desired."[7] Once again, in this view reason is purely instrumental; it can do no more than to serve the passions.

This departure from the ancient understanding of human nature rests upon Hobbes's rejection of the ancient understanding of nature itself. The ancient hope that the passions could be musically moderated with a view to the rule of reason is based upon the belief that such an arrangement in the soul does not frustrate but rather fulfills human nature by allowing the satisfaction of the soul's natural longing to experience moral nobility and philosophic insight. This belief in turn depends upon the ancient conviction that the objects of man's moral and philosophic longing are real. But for Hobbes this is not the case. For him reason can do no more than serve the passions because there is nothing beyond the passions for reason to perceive.

According to Hobbes there is no such thing as "a right Reason constituted by Nature." That is, there are no standards of virtue and vice, of noble and base, inherent in the nature of things for reason to apprehend. On the contrary, our thoughts about such things, far from providing a basis for the moderating of our passions, are in fact nothing more than reflections of our passions: what a man calls good is merely the object of his appetite; what he calls evil the object of his aversion. But Hobbes goes even further. Not only is there no moral order in the nature of things, there is no order at all. Thus he writes that there is "nothing in the world Universall but Names; for the things named, are every one of them Individuall and Singular."[8]

For Hobbes, because an intelligible order to the whole does not exist, there can be nothing in man which naturally longs for it, and hence the ancient attempt to foster happiness by cultivating such longings through graceful music is doomed to failure. One might say, then, that the disappearance of music in early modern political philosophy follows from the disappearance of the soul, at least as it was understood by the ancients: an element of human nature transcending the passions, attracted to things the enjoyment of which requires the quieting of the passions. On Hobbes's understanding, the ancient musical-political undertaking must fail because there is nothing in man inclined by nature to respond to the things depicted in the graceful music of the *Republic* and the *Politics*: the nobility of virtue and the beautiful intelligibility of nature. For Hobbes, then, happiness is defined not as the enjoyment of such things, which requires the calmness of the passions, but rather as simply the gratification of the passions. "Felicity," he writes, "is a continuall progress of the desire, from one object to another."[9]

On the basis of his fundamental agreement with the Machiavellian view of human nature, Hobbes concludes with Machiavelli that the ancient political teaching "was rather a dream than a science."[10] He thus replaces the ancient politics of virtue with a politics much more likely to succeed because it is based upon a proper understanding of human nature, a politics based upon the satisfaction of man's passions, and in particular his most powerful passions which, according to Hobbes, are the desires for one's own preservation and comfort.

Hobbes contends that the end of political life is nothing so elevated as the cultivation of human excellence but rather merely the safety of the people, understood not as "bare Preservation" alone but as including "all other Contentments of life, which every man by lawfull Industry, without danger, or hurt, to the Common-wealth, shall acquire to himselfe."[11] On this understanding political health is reducible to simple concord or peace, the necessary condition of comfortable self-preservation, and does not require, as it does for Plato and Aristotle, the nobility of soul in citizens fostered by music education.[12]

This is not to say that Hobbes presents his political teaching as utterly indifferent to virtue. On the contrary, a certain superficial similarity between Hobbes's commonwealth and Socrates' city in speech is suggested precisely by the attention Hobbes pays to virtue, as well as his advocacy of government censorship as a means of inculcating it. Yet this similarity remains merely superficial because Hobbes, following Machiavelli, understands virtue very differently than the ancients. Thus Hobbes criticizes the ancients for mistakenly thinking the moral virtues desirable in themselves when in fact they are only "the means of peaceable, sociable, and comfortable living."[13] With Hobbes as with Machiavelli virtue is understood as a mere instrument in the service of the satisfaction of the passions, little more than an enlightened material self-interest.

It might be expected that, in spite of this lowering of the ends of political life, a place still might remain in Hobbes's thought for the musical education of the ancients. Plato and Aristotle, after all, argue that such an education is useful not only with a view to the lofty aims of the best regime but also with a view to regime stability and public peace, the more mundane ends that interest Hobbes. Thus, it would seem that even a Hobbesian political order requires some restraint of the passions, if only as a means of preserving the peace upon which a more secure enjoyment of the objects of desire depends.

Yet Hobbes remains true to his understanding of human nature, and therefore grounds whatever restraints he places on the passions in the passions themselves. Abandoning musical character formation, he instead turns to what historian Paul Rahe has aptly termed "political architecture."[14] That is, in Hobbes's thought the internal restraints that the ancients tried futilely to erect within the soul are replaced by external restraints, by institutions that use passion to restrain passion.

In Hobbes's commonwealth men will be moved to do their duty not by any appeal to the virtue-loving and knowledge-loving element in their souls but rather their desire for material well-being, not by

moral education but by the promise of reward and the threat of punishment. Hobbes seeks to secure obedience to the laws of nature,
which are conducive to man's preservation, through the institution
of an all-powerful sovereign, the greatness of whose capacity to reward and punish is so obvious that few, if any, subjects will mistakenly calculate that their interests are better served by disobedience.
Nor does Hobbes resort to moral education of rulers as a means of
minimizing the possibility that they will abuse their great power and
thus threaten the comfortable self-preservation of the subjects.
Hobbes instead responds to this concern by recommending the form
of government he believes will maximize the sovereign's selfish interest in the tranquility and prosperity of the whole commonwealth:
monarchy.[15]

Locke

Locke's political teaching dispenses with the classical belief in the
political importance of music for essentially the same reasons. Like
Hobbes, Locke builds upon the Machiavellian and Glauconian psychology which posits the natural subjection of reason to passion.
God, he writes, has given men "reason to make use of" the world "to
the best advantage of Life, and convenience."[16] Once again, reason is
made the handmaid of the passions and is therefore thought incapable
of having inclinations of its own, the satisfaction of which requires
and justifies the calming of the passions by music. Accompanying this
notion is the belief that nature leaves virtue "unendowed," utterly
bereft of natural attractiveness.[17] Locke teaches the impossibility of
the "harmony between duty and pleasure" that the ancients hoped to
establish through the musical calming of passion and cultivation of
reason.[18]

In light of this understanding of human nature, Locke, like
Hobbes, abandons as unworkable the ancient politics of virtue and
advocates instead a politics that satisfies our most powerful passions,

the desires for life and comfort. Locke says that civil society is instituted with a view to human beings' "comfortable, safe, and peaceable living one amongst another, in a secure Enjoyment of their Properties." Hence, the "*Municipal Laws* of Countries . . . are only so far right, as they are founded on the Law of Nature," a standard of conduct that looks not to the musically cultivated, distinctly human excellence displayed in moral and intellectual activity but only to "the Peace and Preservation of all Mankind."[19]

Locke, no less thoroughgoing than Hobbes in his application of his view of human nature to his entire political teaching, refuses to rely on character formation even to attain these more modest ends. Like Hobbes, Locke employs not internal restraints depending on reason but external restraints depending on passion. The citizens' preservation is to be secured not by some hopeless attempt to reform the soul so that desire will submit to intellect but rather by the creation of laws accompanied by penalties up to and including death.[20] Nor does Locke rely on musical character formation to ensure that those who govern will not use their power contrary to the comfortable self-preservation of the citizens. Rather, like Hobbes, he looks to institutions that use passion to check passion: an executive power subject to law and to a legislative assembly, the members of which are themselves subject to law by means of their short tenure in office.[21]

Montesquieu

Montesquieu's political teaching is developed along the same amusical lines. Like his English counterparts, he holds that the dominant force in human nature is passion, not reason. He thus implicitly denies the ancient belief in the possibility of subjecting passion to reason by means of a moderating musical education.

In Chapter 2 of Book 1 of *The Spirit of the Laws* Montesquieu offers a short history of the state of nature, man's prepolitical condition, intended to illuminate the "laws of nature" that "derive uniquely from the constitution of our being." The first of these laws is "peace," since man's first concern would have been "the preservation of his being." The second is "the one inspiring him to seek nourishment." The third is the natural attraction of the two sexes to each other. The fourth is the "desire to live in society." This last law of nature, however, emerges only after men have "succeeded in gaining knowledge," which, unlike "feelings," does not "belong to men from the outset." Man's "first ideas," Montesquieu argues, "would not be speculative" but would be concerned with his own material well-being.[22]

Feelings or passions emerge earlier and are felt more immediately than reason and are therefore, it seems, more deeply rooted in human nature than reason. For Montesquieu, as for Hobbes and Locke, human nature can be understood—at least for political purposes—as fundamentally passionate.

Montesquieu, like the other early modern political philosophers, is led by this understanding of human nature to advocate a politics which seeks to satisfy the passions rather than one which, seeking to foster virtue, requires the musical calming of the passions. He first suggests this view in the opening chapter of *The Spirit of the Laws*, where he indicates that "the laws of morality" are the province of philosophers, but not of legislators. He further develops this idea in his account of the transition from the state of nature through primitive society to civil society. He claims that laws and government are instituted to stop the state of war that emerges as society develops and that they exist to maintain the existence of society, that is, to prevent a relapse into the state of war in which man's preservation is threatened.[23]

Montesquieu reveals his fundamental agreement with the Hobbesian and Lockean view of politics in his account in Book xi of the best form of government. He remarks that the English constitution "has political liberty for its direct purpose" and later goes on to assert that such a system is "the best kind of government men have been able to devise." Political liberty here appears as *the* political good.

But Montesquieu's definition of political liberty suggests that it is little more than the satisfaction of what he takes to be man's most powerful passion: "Political liberty in a citizen is that tranquility of spirit which comes from the opinion each one has of his security, and in order for him to have this liberty the government must be such that one citizen cannot fear another citizen."[24]

Also like the other early moderns, Montesquieu does not rely on a musical character-forming education even in pursuit of this more modest goal of political life. He too turns to "political architecture," to institutions that check passions by appealing to passions. He hints at this project in his account of the traditional forms of government. There he suggests that aristocracy is stronger than democracy because it relies more on self-interest and less on virtue in securing the enforcement of the law. Similarly, he compares monarchy, which uses "as little virtue as it can," to the "finest machines" which have as few parts and run on as little energy as possible.[25]

For Montesquieu, virtue is politically irrelevant because it cannot dependably secure the end for which government is instituted. Liberty "is present only when power is not abused," but since "it has eternally been observed that any man who has power is led to abuse it," an institutional solution must be sought: "so that one cannot abuse power, power must check power by the arrangement of things." Liberty understood as security requires an elaborate system which, by dividing government power among a number of actors, keeps citizens secure in their lives and properties.[26]

The early moderns, to sum up, reject the ancient claim of the political importance of music because they reject the understanding of human nature and the purpose of politics upon which that claim is based. For the ancients, the soul naturally longs for and finds its final happiness in the activities of moral virtue and philosophy. Thus, their best regime fosters such happiness by means of a musical character formation that cultivates these natural longings while calming the unruly passions that impede their satisfaction. The moderns, however, abandon such an understanding of happiness, and the role of music in fostering it, in light of their belief that passion naturally and necessarily rules in man and that therefore morality and philosophy have no natural attractiveness. On this view, the power of music's charming orderliness cannot reasonably be expected successfully to impose on man a way of life that is contrary to his nature, and therefore the ancient politics of virtue is doomed to failure. The ancient account of a best regime that fosters human excellence through music education is thus abandoned as utopian and replaced with a political order that strives for ends and utilizes means more consistent with man's passionate nature.

This amusical teaching did not, however, prove pleasing to all ears. In Jean-Jacques Rousseau, the modern politics of comfortable self-preservation evoked not admiration but rather a "passionate and still unforgettable protest." Recoiling in disgust from what he regarded as the "degradation of man" in modern politics, Rousseau attempted a return to the ancient "world of virtue and the city."[27] Thus, he returned to a concern with the political uses of music.

❧ 5 ❧

Rousseau's Music of
Passionate Patriotism

USIC AS A POLITICAL FORCE reappears in the thought of
Jean-Jacques Rousseau. Rousseau had an avid interest in
music. He wrote over four hundred articles on the subject for Diderot's *Encyclopedia* and later compiled them in his own
Complete Dictionary of Music.[1] He composed operas, worked as a
music copyist, and even devised a new system of music notation.
Indeed, one commentator suggests that music "perhaps claimed more
[of Rousseau's] attention throughout his life than any other" topic.[2]

Rousseau's understanding of music's power over the soul is re-
markably similar to that of the ancients. In his *Essay on the Origin of
Languages* he reveals that, like Plato and Aristotle, he views music as
a kind of "representation" of the passions, a sign of the "affections" or
"feelings."[3] And like the ancients he thinks music able to "excite in
us the emotions which it expresses, whose image we recognize in it."

Also like his predecessors, Rousseau attributes music's emotional
power primarily to the melody of a song and not to its words.[4] The
language of melody, he contends, "though inarticulate, is lively, ardent,
passionate; and it has a hundred times the power of speech itself." In
this light Rousseau claims that even instrumental music, the music
of "the orchestra," "excites" certain "movements" in the heart.

74

Rousseau's interest in music is also related to his political thought (the last chapter of the *Essay on the Origin of Languages,* which is subtitled, *Which Treats of Melody and Musical Imitation,* is titled: "Relationship of Languages to Government"). Rousseau's return to the ancient understanding of music is intimately related to his return to the ancient understanding of the purpose of politics: he embraces the conviction that politics can and should aim for something lofty.[5] He thus rejects the modern attempt to found politics on material self-interest and is alarmed and disgusted by modern politics' inattention to civic virtue, remarking with distress that while "ancient politicians incessantly talked about morals and virtue, those of our time talk only of business and money."[6] Rousseau looks not to the comfortable self-preservation of the commercial republic but rather to the self-sacrificing public spiritedness of the virtuous republic. Sparta and Rome are his models of the good city.[7]

Yet this observation in itself indicates that there is a limit to how far Rousseau's teaching follows the ancients'. Sparta, which Rousseau praises so ardently, is criticized by Aristotle for mistaking courage for the whole of virtue, and Rome would have received the same condemnation. It comes as no surprise, then, that Rousseau's conclusions about music's power over the soul differ from the ancients'.

Rousseau recognizes with Plato and Aristotle that music's power to imitate passions can be used to calm the soul. He points out that music, though it operates by means of motion, can nonetheless imitate "repose": "Sleep, the calm of night, even silence enter into musical pictures." He departs radically from the ancients, however, insofar as his constant focus is on music's ability to excite the passions. The virtuous or public-spirited politics Rousseau admires is based not on the cultivation of reason, which according to Rousseau is actually destructive of healthy politics but instead upon intensity of passion. Therefore, music's contribution to politics is found in its ability to agitate rather than to still the passions.[8]

The Musical Passions of the Heart

Rousseau's account of music begins with Chapter 12 of the *Essay on the Origin of Languages*, "The Origin of Music and Its Relations." He opens his investigation by contending that the sounds emitted by the first human beings capable of vocal communication were "formed" by "the respective passions that dictated them," so that they were accompanied by "ordinary or unusual tones" and were "more or less sharply accented" depending upon the nature of the feeling to which they were joined. For example, anger "produces menacing cries articulated by the tongue and the palate, while tenderness has a softer voice and is expressed by the glottis."

Rousseau's use of terms such as "accent" and "articulation" implies that these primitive, passionate vocal communications were in some sense musical in nature. He makes this explicit when he contends that the recurring patterns of "measure and rhythm" and the "melodious modulations of accent" dictated by the passions gave birth to poetry, music, and language simultaneously. Or, more accurately, they gave birth to a form of vocal communication that was simultaneously poetic, musical, and linguistic, for Rousseau insists that poetry, music, and language were not originally distinct. He claims that "the first discourses were the first songs" and that the seeming plurality of poetry, music, and language in fact formed, in the beginning, a unity. Rousseau refers to the three as if they were a single entity, saying "that was the only language" that existed at the time.

As Rousseau proceeds, he makes more clear what he means by asserting that the original human language was musical. It was, he suggests, characterized by "melody," which he understands simply as "rhythm and sounds." And the forms of these primal melodies, again, were the result of the influence of the passions of the heart upon the movements of the voice. "At first," Rousseau argues, "there was no music but melody and no other melody than the varied sounds of speech. Accents constituted singing, quantity constituted measure, and one spoke as much by natural sounds and rhythms as by articulations and words."

But not all languages are equally musical. The musical-poetical language Rousseau discusses arose in the south, where the bountifulness of the climate made survival relatively easy. As a result, southern languages express the yearnings of the "heart," specifically the longing for romantic attachment to a person of the opposite sex. Such languages were spoken by the "impassioned voice" and therefore were "sonorous" and "accented." In contrast, the languages of the north are unmusical and incapable of expressing passionate feeling. Due to the harshness of the climate, they express the need to cooperate to provide bodily necessities. As a result, northern languages aimed "not to make someone feel something" but to "make him understand" and thus were characterized more by the "clarity" of "distinct articulation" than the "vigor" of "accents." All modern languages have, for reasons to be discussed later, evolved in the direction of this unmusical northern speech. For this reason, Rousseau ridicules contemporary scholars, orators, and musicians who try to attain the same level of emotional power in music as was achieved by the ancient Greeks, whose tongue he contends was very musical.

As these considerations suggest, the forms of communication to which we moderns refer by the terms "music" and "language" are radically different from the original musical language of the first southern peoples. Our speech lacks melody, and as a result, Rousseau argues later, so does our music. Modern music is dominated by modern harmony, the simultaneous sounding of tones to produce chords, rather than melody understood as the successive sounding of tones in imitation of the passion-inspired voice. Hence, Rousseau asserts that song and speech have the same source rather than that they were the same thing, because it would be grossly misleading for a modern reader to imagine this original melodic language as a combination of modern amelodic language with modern amelodic music.[9] Such a combination would be, for Rousseau, a ridiculous monstrosity, utterly lacking the passionate qualities of the original music he describes in this chapter.

Rousseau proceeds in Chapter 13, "On Melody," to offer a criticism of his contemporaries' failure to understand the true basis of music's capacity to please and to move us. A painting's ability to express and excite certain passions, Rousseau claims, is "not at all due to the colors," which may give some pleasure of the sense, but the "drawing," the "representation" of certain "objects" which move our affections. Similarly, "the power of music over our souls is not at all the work of sounds," however physically agreeable they may be, but of the arrangement of sounds in a melodic imitation of the passions: "The role of melody in music is precisely that of drawing in a painting. This is what constitutes the strokes and figures, of which the harmony and the sounds are merely the colors."[10] Rousseau's focus is on intelligible form over matter, on what transcends matter over matter itself, on the spiritual over the physical. This is in keeping with his later suggestion that the realm of moral passions itself transcends man's merely physical nature, which is in turn the basis of his complaints about the reductionism of modern philosophy.

On the basis of this understanding, Rousseau contemptuously dismisses the ideas of Jean-Philippe Rameau, the music theorist and composer of immensely popular French operas, who contended that music's power was based on harmony's grounding in the laws of physics. Rousseau, disdaining what he takes to be the poverty of this account of music, asks what we should say to a painter and to a musician "sufficiently devoid of feeling and taste" so "stupidly" to limit "the pleasurable character of" their respective arts to their "mere mechanics," the one by attributing painting's power to colors and the other by considering "harmony the sole source of the great effects of music." Rousseau's response: "Let us consign the first to house painting and the other to doing French opera."

Ultimately, Rousseau's complaint is that Rameau's theory of music rests upon an impoverished philosophy of the arts and of human nature. If there were no more to music and painting than "combining sounds to please the ear" and "combining colors to please the eye," both would be natural sciences rather than fine arts. "Imitation alone raises them to this level," and painting and music are made "imitative" by "Drawing" and "Melody" respectively. There is, Rousseau suggests, more to man than physical reactions to physical stimuli. Imitation raises the fine arts to a level higher than that of the natural sciences because the moral passions, which are the objects of artistic imitation, are higher than the physical phenomena, which are the objects of scientific investigation. Thus man, insofar as he is capable of experiencing the passions of the heart, somehow transcends physical or material nature. And therefore a philosophy of music, and of man, that claims all things "must be traced to physical causes," and thus denies the "stirrings of the spirit" by holding that nothing except sensation is involved in music's effect on men, must be woefully wrongheaded.

Such philosophy is not only mistaken about but actually harmful to music and to man. Rousseau closes Chapter 15 by commenting that "in this century when all the operations of the soul have to be materialized, and deprived of all morality and human feeling, I am deluded if the new philosophy does not become as destructive of good taste as of virtue." This new materialistic philosophy destroys good taste because only music that imitates the passion-inspired voice—that is, melody—is "delightful" and "voluptuous." Only it can "charm and soften" the listener. In comparison, the merely physical sensation produced by a series of sounds or chords—that is, non-imitative and non-melodic music—is hadly pleasant at all. It may amuse one for a moment but will soon grow tiresome. But on Rousseau's account, this feeble kind of music is all that modern philosophy can offer. In Chapter 17 he characterizes as "An Error of Musicians Harmful to Their Art" the tendency of modern musicians to "assimilate" their art "to purely physical impressions." The more they do so, he contends, "the farther they get from its source and the more they deprive it of its primitive energy. In dropping its oral tone and sticking exclusively to the establishment of harmonies, music becomes noisier to the ear and less pleasing to the heart. As soon as it stops singing it stops speaking. And then, with all its accord and all its harmony it will have no more effect upon us."

Materialistic philosophy undermines virtue by assaulting the beliefs necessary to sustain virtue as Rousseau understands it: selfless dedication to the good of the political community, extending even to a willingness to risk and even sacrifice one's own life in its defense. After all, if men believe themselves to be nothing but matter, then they will likely take seriously only their material interests and thus will not be capable of the heroic citizenship of which Rousseau so warmly approves. On the contrary, the materialistic understanding of music and man leads ineluctably to the politics of comfortable self-preservation that Rousseau rejects.

Music, Culture, and Human Nature

Rousseau's teaching initially appears ambiguous on whether the emotional power of music is grounded in human nature and therefore universally able to speak to the soul or is merely the product of convention and therefore relative to culture. He seems at first to adopt the latter view. While sounds do convey a physical pleasure that is universally experienced, that pleasure has little effect on the soul, which can only be moved by sounds "enlivened by melodious inflections that are familiar" to the listener. Music, then, "is a tongue for which one needs a dictionary." This passage suggests that the emotional power of music is largely, perhaps entirely, culturally relative. The power of melody appears to depend upon cultural learning, and thus particular melodies appear to possess no natural, universal ability to move the passions.

The development of Rousseau's argument, however, suggests a certain modification of this initial assertion about melody's status, implying that there is a natural basis for melodic communication of the passions after all. After indicating that melody is dependent upon culture or convention, Rousseau proceeds to suggest that it is nevertheless not conventional in the same way as harmony. He states that harmony is a "more difficult matter" because it is "only conventionally beautiful" and "does not in any way please the unpracticed ear," the taste for it requiring long exposure. Hence, "to the uncultured ear, our consonances are merely noise." Indeed, harmony is actually repugnant to nature. The multiplication of simultaneously sounding tones characteristic of modern harmony, Rousseau claims, obscures the natural beauty of simple sounds and thus destroys the pleasure of hearing them.

If sounds, on the one hand, are purely natural, and harmony, on the other, is purely conventional, it could appear that melody occupies a position somewhere in between. If the uncultured ear regards our harmonies as mere noise, then perhaps it does not simply so regard foreign, unfamiliar melodies. Perhaps that is why Rousseau, even in the middle of his argument that the effect of melody depends on familiarity, implicitly concedes a certain universal emotional power to the melodies of a particular culture: "The songs most beautiful to us will only moderately move those to whom they are quite unfamiliar." Again, if sound is agreeable to human nature, and if harmony is a convention repugnant to human nature, could melody fall somewhere in between? Could it be a convention that is not repugnant to nature, as harmony is, but rather in accord with it? And could it be in this sense partly natural and partly conventional?

The existence of some natural grounding for melody is explicitly confirmed in Chapter 16, where Rousseau asserts that "Nature inspires songs, not accords; she speaks of melody, not harmony." Melody, he contends, announces the presence of another being like oneself and in so doing spontaneously generates an excitement in the soul. Music can "relate man to man," and it "always gives us some idea of our kind." In contrast to painting, which "is often dead and inanimate," "vocal signs" immediately "announce to you a being like yourself. They are, so to speak, the voice of the soul. If you hear them in the wilderness, they tell you you are not there alone." "Birds whistle; man alone sings," Rousseau continues, "and one cannot hear either singing or a symphony without immediately acknowledging the presence of another intelligent being."

Rousseau goes beyond claiming that, generally speaking, melodic communication of emotions is natural to human beings. He suggests that particular melodic forms are naturally and universally imitations of particular emotions. The passions of the heart and the melodies by which they are communicated are not merely cultural constructs, but rather grounded in nature. If, as Rousseau argues, melody can, "in the wilderness," that is, apart from civilization and the shared cultural language found in it, announce the presence of an intelligent, sensitive being like oneself, then it must possess some communicative power that is natural and universal. Unless human beings as human beings naturally share certain passions of the heart and the melodic means of expressing them, vocal signs heard in the wilderness would not signify anything unless they happened to be those of one's own cultural group.

Rousseau again suggests, at the beginning his account of the origins of music in Chapter 12, that melody is a universal and natural language of the passions of the heart. He identifies "melody" with "rhythm and sounds" and then goes on to claim that the original musical communication was carried on by means of "natural sounds and rhythms," that is, natural melody. But on Rousseau's account such communication could not be wholly conventional. After all, the earliest humans were able to move each other by it, and yet they had no shared, familiar conventions. Far from being merely a product of culture, musical communication of the natural passions made possible the uniting of previously asocial human beings into the first primitive culture.

Rousseau makes his understanding of melody most clear in Chapter 14, when he explains more extensively how melody "gives music its power of representation, and song its power over sensitive hearts." It does so, Rousseau argues, by "imitating the inflections of the voice." "Melody expresses pity, cries of sorrow and joy, threats and groans. All the vocal signs of passion are within its domain. It imitates the tones of language, and the twists produced in every idiom by certain psychic acts." This passage implies a universal and thus natural appeal of melody. Rousseau speaks not of the various vocal signs of passion of the various cultures but rather of "the vocal signs of passion" simply, as if these signs are always and everywhere the same and intelligible to everybody. Even more telling is the statement that certain movements of soul produce the same twists of tone "in every idiom," that is, in every language and culture.[11]

Nevertheless, even in these arguments stressing the natural status of melody, Rousseau includes statements pointing back to his initial assertion of melody's dependence on convention. He states in Chapter 16, for example, that compared to painting, "music is more dependent on human art." We are thus brought back to the idea that melody is both natural and conventional, that it is, if one may be permitted the expression, a natural convention. Melody is conventional insofar as it is the product of development beyond the original state of nature. But it is natural insofar as that very development seems somehow intended by nature itself, for Rousseau suggests both that there is a natural directedness toward musical communication of the passions of the heart and that the experience of those passions represents a fulfillment of our nature.

Again, if melody or musical language is in this sense natural, then the passions of the heart must be as well, for Rousseau holds that the latter give rise to the former. But this is to suggest that man is by nature intended to live in a certain kind of society, the possibility of which requires some development beyond his original, solitary, nonrational state. This understanding is contrary to what most people imagine, with some justification, that Rousseau teaches: he himself denies man's natural sociability, and he explicitly asserts in the *Second Discourse* that "moral love," which in the *Essay* is called the passions of the heart, "is an artificial sentiment born of the usage of society" and founded on ideas about "merit or beauty that a savage is not capable of having."[12]

Nevertheless, the argument of the *Essay* implies that man has a natural directedness toward society and the development of the passions of the heart. Rousseau says, for example, that "as soon as one man was recognized by another as a sentient, thinking being similar to himself, the desire or need to communicate his feelings and thoughts made him seek the means to do so." Here a certain level of sociability seems spontaneous, given the requisite development. Rousseau then proceeds to say that the sensible signs used in the earliest communication were not devised rationally but by instinct. But this is as much as to say that our ability to communicate, and thus our sociability, is supported by nature.

The *Second Discourse* similarly implies this natural directedness of man toward some at least rudimentary society. There Rousseau suggests that the artificial society in which man comes to live at a certain point in his progress beyond his original state, and hence the artificial sentiments that he comes to experience there, represents a fulfillment of his nature. That man's nature might require some conventional development to be fully realized is indicated in the first place by Rousseau's account of pity, which is classed with our desire for our own well-being as one of the "first and simplest operations of the human soul" and is explicitly referred to as "a natural sentiment."[13] Yet this natural sentiment evidently requires some intellectual development before it can come into play. Rousseau writes in the *Essay* that though "pity is native to the human heart, it would remain eternally quiescent unless it were activated by imagination." But imagination, which depends upon the possession of "a great deal of acquired knowledge," is not active in man in his original state. Pity, although it is explicitly identified as natural, nonetheless appears to have the same quasi-natural, quasi-artificial status as the "moral needs" or "passions of the heart" discussed in the *Essay*. One thus suspects that the latter, though they are first introduced as artificial, are no less natural than the former.[14]

Other aspects of the argument of the *Second Discourse* indicate that this is the case. At the beginning of that work, Rousseau suggests that in his account the reader will find "the age at which [he] would desire [his] species had stopped" developing.[15] Such a statement implies that the best state for man would not be his original state in which he was utterly without conventions but rather some point of development beyond that first situation. After all, to say that there is a point at which we wish the species had stopped developing is tacitly to acknowledge the goodness of some development.

Later in the *Second Discourse*, Rousseau confirms that this desirable stopping point is the stage at which man communicates his passions melodically, which suggests that this stage, though a result of progress beyond the state of nature, is nevertheless a fulfillment of human nature. ˙Rousseau first implies as much in his reference to the original man, who lived in utter isolation and entirely by "blind inclination," as merely "nascent man." Prior to some development of his reason and sociability, it seems, man was not yet fully man. Rousseau further indicates that human beings' earliest experience of living together was accompanied by the "first developments of the heart" and gave rise to "the sweetest sentiments known to men: conjugal love and paternal love." He further praises "this period of the development of human faculties" as "the best for man" and says that it "must have been the happiest and most durable epoch." Rousseau indicates, perhaps more directly, that the stage of man's development during which melody arose is natural, by the claim that it seems that "the human race was made to remain in it always," a claim that provokes the question: By what, if not nature, is man made to remain in savage society?[16]

Just as Rousseau, in the *Essay*, presents passionate melody as occupying a partly natural and partly conventional middle ground that is superior to the purely natural and purely conventional extremes of mere sounds and harmony, respectively, so the nascent society in which melodic communication emerges is presented by the *Second Discourse* as a "golden mean between the indolence of the primitive state and the petulant activity of our vanity."[17]

Melody, Politics, and Modern Decadence

In the "Preface" to the *Second Discourse*, Rousseau indicates that he undertakes his investigation of man's nature with a view to discovering "natural right," a standard by which one can correctly judge contemporary political societies.[18] As we have seen, Rousseau's arguments in both the *Essay* and the *Second Discourse* point to his belief that man's nature fully emerges not in his original state of utter solitude but rather in the simple society in which the passions of the heart, especially "moral" love, are experienced and communicated through the melody of the impassioned voice. This stage of man's development, then, serves as Rousseau's standard of judgment.[19]

The best political community will not be one in which men are as solitary as they can be consistent with the good order upon which the satisfaction of their selfish desire for comfortable self-preservation depends. (Such a position would, of course, be more in line with the thought of the early moderns.) Rather, the best political community for Rousseau will be one that engages the passions of the heart, one in which the city inspires the same ardent dedication in the citizen that the beloved inspires in the lover.

Rousseau suggests, in a number of passages in his writings, that an imperfect version of the natural happiness of nascent society can, through politics, be realized at a later stage in man's development. The *Letter to d'Alembert*, for example, claims that ancient tragedy depicted "situations drawn from the political concerns we no longer have" and the "simple and natural sentiments which no longer move anyone."[20] This implies the possibility of a politics based upon natural sentiments, upon the melodically communicated moral passions. Moreover, the *Second Discourse*'s dedication "To the Republic of Geneva" indicates that there can be a political arrangement "most approximate to natural law" and thus "most favorable to . . . the happiness of individuals."[21]

Such a political community, Rousseau indicates, will be characterized by freedom and to that extent will reproduce the natural liberty enjoyed in the state of nature. It will, to be sure, require virtuous self-sacrifice on the part of its citizens. Yet such self-sacrifice will not be experienced as servitude. Flowing from love, self-sacrifice will be agreeable to the passions, just as the service given to the family in nascent society is rendered agreeable by the sweetness of conjugal and paternal love. Moreover, Rousseau suggests in the *Essay* that the passionate patriotism of the good political society, no less than the moral love of nascent society, depends upon the melodic communication of the desires of the heart.

In the final chapter of the *Essay*, "Relationship of Languages to Government," Rousseau argues that melody is necessary for freedom. He observes that only "sonorous, prosodic," and "harmonious" tongues, such as that of the classical Greeks, are "favorable to liberty." Amusical language, in contrast, is useless with a view to making "oneself understood to the people assembled" and is therefore "slavish."

Rousseau reveals what he means by liberty, and how it is dependent on melody, in Chapter 12, the beginning of his account of music. Rousseau's argument in that chapter leads to the conclusion that the first tales, speeches, and laws were expressed in the musical-poetic language he attributes to the first southern peoples. And later in the chapter he implies that this language was the basis of political order among these early humans who first uttered it, that it alone gave force to the law. "Considering the way in which the earliest societies were bound together," he asks, "is it surprising that the first stories were in verse and the first laws were sung?" The first human communities existed without the benefit of a modern state enforcing the laws through overwhelming coercive power. As a result, the first laws had to carry a kind of persuasiveness of their own, which they could only have through the capacity of music to move passions. The first southern peoples were free, then, insofar as among them the individual member's conformity to the common way of life was the result not of a dread of punishment but rather of a passion for their way of life, excited by the musical language in which the community's laws and tales were expressed.

This understanding of the relationship between music and freedom Rousseau advances explicitly in Chapter 20. He contends that while "eloquence was necessary" in "ancient times" because persuasion then "played the role of public force," today, "when public force has replaced persuasion," eloquence is useless. Modern politics, it seems, involves a coercive imposition of the ruler's desires on the subjects. It is, therefore, fundamentally different from the kind of politics made possible by musical language, a politics in which the desire of the ruler is shared by the whole community because it has been presented to them and inspired within the soul of each by means of the persuasive power of melody.

We are now in a position better to grasp Rousseau's comment, noted earlier, that the "new philosophy," materialism, is "as destructive of good taste as of virtue." Materialism destroys good musical taste by encouraging a movement away from use of melody's "delightful" imitation and inspiration of the passions and toward a reliance on mere physical sensations, which quickly grow tiresome. Materialism destroys virtue by denying the beliefs necessary to disregarding one's material interests in favor of the good of the community.

Now we see in addition that materialism destroys virtue by first destroying good taste: its undermining of music contributes to the death of virtue.

Rousseau's account of the great gulf between the politics of the ancients and the moderns points to the question: How was melody—and freedom—lost? Rousseau answers this question in Chapter 19, his account of "How Music Has Degenerated." He identifies four factors that explain the decline of melody. The first of these is the rise of philosophy. For Rousseau, it is no accident that ancient Greece, whose original language he regards as the model of the power of melodic speech, came to be "full of sophists and philosophers" at the same time as it began to lack "famous musicians." The disappearance of the latter was caused by the multiplication of the former, for in "cultivating the art of convincing, the art of arousing the emotions was lost."

The flourishing of philosophy, Rousseau suggests, depends upon, and therefore fosters the refinement of, speech as a tool of rational discourse. Thus the "study of philosophy and the progress of reason" led to the perfecting of "grammar." The necessary consequence of this progress, however, was to "deprive language of its vital, passionate quality which made it so singable." Thus to make language an instrument of intellectual clarity is to guarantee its emotional flaccidity. But this in turn necessarily leads to the degeneration of music, the loss of its power to express and inspire passion. To wield such power, after all, music must be melodic, an imitation of the natural inflections of the passionate human voice. But when those inflections are no longer present in the language, they cannot be imitated in the music, and the nature of music comes to be determined by technical acoustic considerations. Rousseau argues that "to the degree that language improved, melody" came to be governed by "the calculus of intervals" rather than "nicety of inflection," with the result that music "imperceptibly lost its former energy" and "stopped producing the marvels

it had produced when it was merely the accent and harmony of poetry and gave to it the power over the passions that speech subse-
quently exercised only on reason."

Second, Rousseau argues that "servitude soon joined forces with
philosophy" in causing music's decay. Greece was conquered by
Rome, and "in fetters" she "lost the fire that warms only free spirits,
and in praising her tyrants, she never recovered the style in which she
had sung her heroes." This led in turn to the third cause: the influence of the conquerors' "less musical tongue" continued to diminish
"whatever harmony and accent remained in the language" and thus
"did harm to the music" that adopted it. Finally, the stroke fatal to
melodic music was delivered by the triumph of a language utterly
unable to express or inspire the passions of the heart. As a result of
the barbarian conquest of Rome, "every ear" gradually "became accustomed to the rude" and "expressionless" language of "these coarse
men engendered by the North." And the ultimate outcome of this was
a singing "consisting solely of volume and duration of sounds" and
thus completely "devoid of melody," lacking all imitative power.

This loss of melody, moreover, gave rise to the modern harmonic
music Rousseau so deplores. The necessarily unsatisfying practice
of amelodic music finally led musicians to a technique by which, so
they thought, the charm of music could, "with the help of consonances," be recovered. Harmony was introduced and melody as it
originally existed was forgotten, replaced by an arbitrary and
unimitative counterfeit. As musicians gradually allowed themselves
to be "governed entirely according to this novelty," Rousseau writes,
the succession of chords came to dictate the movement of voices, and
that movement "usurped the name of melody," though "it was, in effect,
impossible to recognize the traits of its mother in this new melody."
And, having departed so far from its original nature, having lost its
"oral tone," music lost "almost all its energy."

It is interesting to note that in Chapter 18 Rousseau claims in
passing that the degeneration of music occurred as a result of a "natu-

ral change in the character of the tongues." This suggests that the progress of reason, and not the other things mentioned, is the fundamental cause of music's degeneration. Indeed, this original loss of melody as a result of the progress of reason is itself the cause of the conquest that led to the further corruption of music. After all, Rousseau argues in the *First Discourse* that development of the arts and sciences leads to moral corruption, which in turn leads to being conquered by foreigners.[22] The *Essay* sheds additional light on that argument: if the passionate appeal of melodious language is necessary to fostering virtue, understood as selfless commitment to the political community, then the rationalization and demusicalization of language causes weakness in the citizens, a lack of public-spiritedness, which invites, because it cannot resist, attack and subjection.[23]

Rousseau's critique of reason also sheds light on a difference noted at the beginning of this chapter between his account of music and that of his ancient predecessors. Plato and Aristotle think music politically useful because of its ability to calm the passions. Rousseau, in contrast, thinks it politically useful because of its ability to inspire the passions. Plato and Aristotle want to calm the passions with a view to the cultivation of reason, which they believe is conducive to the well-being of both the political community and the individual insofar as it fosters moral and philosophic virtue. Rousseau, of course, agrees that moral virtue is necessary for the well-being of society and the individual. Yet for Rousseau this virtue and this happiness are based not on reason but on passion.

Indeed, for Rousseau political and individual well-being cannot be based on reason, which, according to him, is only a late and rather weak human development: it is not, he explicitly affirms, one of the two passionate operations natural to the human soul, self-interest and pity.[24] Reason is therefore subordinate to passion. This is made clear, in a formulation recalling Hobbes's characterization of reason as merely a scout and spy for the passions, in the *Second Discourse*: it is by the activity of the passions that "reason is perfected; we seek to know only because we desire to have pleasure."[25] Rousseau thus follows the early moderns in their repudiation of the ancient understanding of the relationship of reason and passion;[26] he departs from them in that he does not insist that man's passions are exclusively or fundamentally selfish or asocial.

This is not to say that for Rousseau reason has no role to play in the realization of man's happiness. Clearly it does, for he indicates that the passions of the heart can only be activated after some development of man's mind. Nevertheless, Rousseau departs radically from the ancients in that for him the activity of reason is merely ancillary to the realization of happiness in another sphere—that of the passions of the heart—and is not itself immediately productive of happiness. Put another way, while for the ancients man is fundamentally a rational being whose happiness increases with the excellent exercise of his reason, for Rousseau man is fundamentally a passionate or emotional being, whose experience of happiness through the passions of the heart is fostered by the development of his mind only to a certain point beyond which further intellectual progress is positively harmful.

One wonders at this point why Rousseau's account of the political importance of music is not contained in one of his more prominent, and more explicitly political, works and is consigned instead to a work, the *Essay*, he never published. The answer seems to reside in his ambivalence about the applicability of his teaching to contemporary politics. Rousseau's argument indicates the desirability of a return to the musical politics of the Greeks before the rise of philosophy, a politics that was itself an approximation of the more perfect happiness of nascent society. Such a return would necessitate a reformation of modern music and language, a recovery of the power of melody as an imitation of the passionate voice and a corresponding diminution of the prominence of harmony. Rousseau appears doubtful about whether such a reformation is possible, whether his insight into the dependence of healthy politics on passionate music can be used to improve contemporary politics.

Indeed, on the basis of the *Essay* alone one wonders whether human action can preserve the musical politics to which Rousseau looks as a standard. Rousseau suggests at one point that the decay of music and the accompanying loss of freedom is beyond human control. This decline, he writes, is the result of "a natural change in the character of tongues" and belongs, therefore, "to the vicissitudes of things."

Nevertheless, the *First Discourse* offers some basis for hope. Rousseau indicates that the political and moral weakness resulting from the progress of philosophy can be forestalled by human action because they can be foreseen by human wisdom. He claims that it was "not through stupidity" that simple, virtuous peoples "have preferred other exercises to those of the mind." "They were not unaware that in other lands idle men spent their lives debating about the greatest good, vice and virtue . . . But they considered their morals and learned to disdain their doctrine."[27] Free and virtuous peoples may not understand the role of melody in fostering virtue, but they apparently have prudence enough to eschew philosophy because of the bad political consequences that seem to follow it, and that is sufficient to guarantee the continued vitality of music and language and the survival of freedom.

Rousseau appears equally ambivalent about whether melodic music and language, and the free and happy politics to which they give rise, can be recovered after they have already been lost. On the one hand, the *Essay* powerfully conveys an impression of profound pessimism. Rousseau ends the work with an account of the deplorable state of modern politics and offers no suggestion that the situation can be remedied. Indeed, his comment that "societies have assumed their final form" seems to exclude the possibility of a return to a melodically inspired politics of patriotism and freedom.[28] This position would be in harmony with his claim, advanced in both his "Observations" addressed to the king of Poland and his "Preface" to *Narcisse*, that a corrupted people could never recover its virtue.[29]

One the other hand, a number of passages in Rousseau's writings suggest some grounds for hope. Both the *Essay* and the *Complete Dictionary of Music* indicate that even modern European music retains some ability to move the soul, and in the latter's entry on "Expression" Rousseau indicates the lines along which music should be reformed in order to increase that ability: melody should be derived from oratorical accent, and harmony should be subordinate to melody and never obscure it.[30] He even suggests, in his unpublished *Origin of Melody*, that as a result of such a reformation opera might be able to revive the ancient power of melody.[31] Moreover, that Rousseau thought that such a remelodization and rejuvenation of music might have salutary political consequences is suggested by the following comment from a fragment on "Pronunciation": "For a long time the public is never spoken to except by books, and if something is still to be said to it in a strong voice which interests it, this must be done at the theatre."[32]

The hope suggested by this last passage, however, remained for Rousseau a private thought, for the fragment in question was never published by him.[33] Rousseau's public statement on the political influence of the theater—and, presumably, the part played by music in the theater—is contained in the *Letter to D'Alembert*, the argument of which, as is well known, holds that its influence is unequivocally harmful. It seems, then, that in the end Rousseau's hope that music's power might be restored and used to foster a politically beneficial passionate attachment to our duties was outweighed by his fear that our language is so debilitated that our music likely could do no more than to provide a politically harmful distraction from our duties.

∞ 6 ∞

Nietzsche's Tragic Politics of Music

ROUSSEAU SUGGESTS that in the modern world the only remaining hope—and it is a slim hope—for some renewal of politics lies in music's ability to move the human soul. The person who in the nineteenth century took this idea most seriously, and acted on it most energetically, was Richard Wagner. Indeed, in Wagner Rousseau's almost forlorn hope becomes confident expectation. For Wagner made a career of trying to reshape German culture through the influence of his music dramas.[1]

Wagner's young disciple, Friedrich Nietzsche, sympathized with Wagner's aims and shared his hope of success. Of Wagner's work Nietzsche wrote to a friend, "if only a few hundred people get from this music what I get from it, then we will have a completely new culture."[2] Ultimately it fell to Nietzsche and not Wagner to offer the most systematic exposition of the idea of music as a force for the renewal of a decadent modernity. This exposition is found in Nietzsche's first major work, *The Birth of Tragedy Out of the Spirit of Music*, a book which he explicitly acknowledges was written under Wagner's influence. Hence we turn to Nietzsche's *Birth of Tragedy* to learn his teaching on the relationship of music and politics.[3]

The Politics of Nobility

An examination of Nietzsche's account of music in *The Birth of Trag-edy* suggests that his thought, like Rousseau's, in some sense departs from the early moderns and returns to the ancients. Certainly the importance he accords music is more characteristic of Plato and Aristotle than of Hobbes, Locke, and Montesquieu. Like his ancient predecessors, Nietzsche recognizes but explicitly rejects the view that music is merely for the sake of pleasure. He remarks that those read-ers who "are unable to consider art more than a pleasant sideline, a readily dispensable tinkling of bells that accompanies the 'seriousness of life,'" might well be offended that he takes aesthetic problems so seriously.[4] Such readers, however, are misled, and Nietzsche advises them to learn from his conviction "that art represents the highest task and the truly metaphysical activity of this life." Indeed, near the end of *The Birth of Tragedy* Nietzsche indicates that he, like Plato and Aristotle, believes music's role in politics to be critically important. He invites the attentive and sympathetic reader "to an elevated posi-tion of lonely contemplation." From this peak he observes that the "degeneration and transformation" of the character of the ancient Greeks consequent upon the removal of music from tragedy "calls for serious reflection" on the "fundamental connections" between, on the one hand, "myth" and "tragedy"—both of which depend upon mu-sic—and, on the other hand, "custom" and "the state."

For Nietzsche, as for his predecessors and in contrast to the par-ties to our contemporary disputes, the political importance of music belongs primarily to the music itself, and not the words. Tone, melody, and harmony, he contends, form the essence of the "Diony-sian" music he discusses. Music thus understood is the "primary and universal" language that so powerfully moves the soul. In "its abso-lute sovereignty" it "does not *need*" to be joined to poetic speech, which it "merely *endures*" as a kind of accompaniment. Musical mood, he agrees with Schiller, comes before and gives rise to poetic language, which "can never adequately render" that which is communicated by the music itself.

Moreover, with Nietzsche as with Rousseau, this return to serious consideration of music's power over the soul goes hand in hand with a return to the ancient concern with virtue or excellence or nobility, a longing for a higher human type than that fostered by the politics of the early moderns. Just as Rousseau disdains the bourgeois and laments the modern politician's lack of attention to virtue and excessive attention to commerce, so Nietzsche expresses disgust that, in the work of Euripides and his successors, drama, which before had represented "only grand and beautiful traits," came instead to represent only "the everyday man" and his "craven satisfaction with easy enjoyment." Yet such concerns, for self-preservation and material advantage, are precisely the star by which the early modern thinkers seek to guide politics.

Finally, Nietzsche hopes that the power of music can resurrect culture understood as a unified way of life of a whole people and thus replace the rather thin gruel of community life offered by the liberal politics of the early moderns: each individual pursuing happiness according to his idiosyncratic understanding of it, united—if that is the word—to his fellows only by adherence to laws designed to promote no higher end than the preservation and comfort of all.

The Music of Will

Nevertheless, one is struck most powerfully by the differences between Nietzsche and the ancients. If one disregards the amusical political teaching of the early moderns, in light of which Nietzsche and the ancients appear to have much in common, and simply compares Nietzsche's account of music and politics with that of Plato and Aristotle, a radical opposition emerges. Nietzsche stands with the ancients to the extent that he is mindful of music's power over the soul and the political importance of that power, but he stands in opposi-

tion to the ancients insofar as the kind of music he endorses as politically salutary is radically different from that endorsed by Plato and
Aristotle. This difference can be stated, without oversimplification,
as simply and starkly as this: Plato and Aristotle recommend an orderly music that calms the passions and awakens and strengthens
reason in the soul. Nietzsche, in contrast, recommends a music that
inflames the passions, and he seeks to use such music with a view to
overwhelming or silencing reason.

These differences first come to light in *The Birth of Tragedy* in
Nietzsche's description of what he calls the Apollinian and Dionysian
art impulses of nature. The experiencing of Apollinian art, the ex-
emplification of which is sculpture, Nietzsche compares to the "delight" we find in the "immediate understanding of figures" when
dreaming. The Apollinian art experience is characterized by a state
of contemplation in which one enjoys the beautiful intelligibility of
the Apollinian illusion. Such contemplation, Nietzsche indicates, is
necessarily accompanied by "that calm sea of the soul" the Greeks
called "*sophrosune*," or moderation, by "measured restraint" and "freedom from the wilder emotions."

In contrast, the experience of Dionysian art, the highest manifestation of which is music, "is brought home to us most intimately by
the analogy of intoxication." This experience is characterized not by
freedom from the wilder emotions but possession by them. Thus
Nietzsche points to such examples of the Dionysian experience as the
medieval German dancers of St. John and St. Vitus, singing and danc-
ing from place to place, the Bacchic choruses of the Greeks, and their
more barbaric predecessor, the "orgiastic" Babylonian Sacaea. For
Nietzsche, music gives expression not to intelligible beauty which
induces a contemplative frame of mind but rather to "will," understood as passion or desiring. Hence he quotes with approval from
Schopenhauer's *World as Will and Idea*: "All possible efforts, excite-
ments, and manifestations of will, all that goes on in the heart of man
and that reason includes in the wide, negative concept of feeling," is

expressed in music. In sum, for Nietzsche, when we experience the Apollinian we behold images, but when we experience the Dionysian —that is, when we experience music—we feel forces.

Nietzsche's radical departure from the ancients can also be seen in his account of the musical revolution begun by Beethoven and completed by Wagner. In his essay, "Richard Wagner at Bayreuth," Nietzsche claims that before Wagner music expressed "man's abiding conditions," that is, "mood," or "what the Greeks termed *ethos*." All "deepenings and excesses of feeling were considered 'unethical,'" and therefore the mood expressed and impressed upon the listener, through "a certain homogeneity of form" and a "sustained duration of this homogeneity," was characterized by a kind of repose of the passions, or at least by a freedom from the wilder emotions induced by Dionysian art. Nietzsche says that such music was expected to foster in the listener a "calmer, brighter, more devout, or more penitent state."[5]

This music, however, finally "exhausted itself" after having "presented man's continuing familiar states and moods in hundreds of repetitions," and this opened the door for Beethoven to introduce a kind of music that spoke "a new language, the hitherto forbidden language of passion." Music abandoned the language of *ethos* and took up the language of "*pathos*, of the passionate will." Nevertheless, Beethoven's attachment to the conventions of the older artistic regime prevented him from giving perfect expression to passion. This accomplishment fell to Wagner, whose music, according to Nietzsche, is "the process of feeling and passion made audible," which gives "completely unambiguous utterance" to "every grade and every color of feeling."

Nietzsche clearly approved of this transformation of the character of music. The general theme of "Richard Wagner at Bayreuth" is his admiration for the composer's accomplishments, and in a letter to Erwin Rhode, Nietzsche writes that Wagner's work "is exactly what music is! And that is exactly what I mean by the word 'music' when

I call it Dionysian!"[6] But his approval of this transformation must be regarded as a rejection of the ancient teaching about music and politics. For the old music of *ethos*, whose decline so pleases Nietzsche, and which seeks to induce a certain calmness of mood by means of homogeneity of form, bears a striking resemblance to the music of Socrates' city in speech, which seeks to foster moderation by means of simplicity of rhythm and harmony. Wagner's music, the rise of which is so enthusiastically approved by Nietzsche, and which gives expression to "every grade and color" of passion, is very similar to the panharmonic music banished by Socrates because it indiscriminately depicts every state of soul.[7]

In sum, Nietzsche's musical prescriptions are diametrically opposed to those of the ancients. Socrates banishes from his perfectly just city both excessive laughter and excessive lamentation—and the musical modes appropriate to them. Nietzsche, in contrast, recommends a Dionysian music that gives expression to both excessive pleasure and pain, to "ecstasy" and "agony." Socrates banishes the modes appropriate to symposia, but Nietzsche endorses a music whose effect he likens to intoxication.

Nietzsche's radical new musical prescription is connected to his rejection of the end the ancients had in view for their soul-soothing music: the cultivation of reason. Nietzsche knew of a kind of music capable of expressing Apollinian states and therefore presumably able, like the music of the *Republic*, to foster the calmness of soul necessary to contemplation. He knew further that the proponents of such music expected it, as Socrates expected his music, to produce "an effect similar to that produced by works of plastic art, namely, the arousing of *delight in beautiful forms*." Nietzsche follows Wagner, however, in rejecting such music as "mistaken and degenerate." Real music is characterized not by intelligible beauty but by "emotional power," and its purpose is not to strengthen reason by cultivating its attraction to beautiful order but rather to overwhelm reason's command of the soul. Nietzsche characterizes Dionysian music as intoxicating, and he praises Wagner's music for its ability to produce, by means of the powerful "thrill" it sends "through every fibre" and "every nerve," "such a sustained feeling of being *carried away*."[8]

Nietzsche departs so radically from the ancients in the character and aim of the music he endorses because his understanding of man differs fundamentally from that held by the ancients. Nietzsche's rejection of Socrates' policy of banning the instruments and music of the satyr Marsyas and keeping those of Apollo stems from his disagreement with Socrates over which of these two figures better represents human nature.

According to Nietzsche, the ecstatically passionate Dionysian experience "wells from the innermost depths of man," and the satyr, the Dionysian reveller, is "the true human being," the "archetype of man, the embodiment of his highest and most intense emotions." In contrast, Socrates argues that reason is the distinctively human element in man. He indicates in Book x of the *Republic* that the passions, far from representing man's inmost depths, are unnatural accumulations that obscure the soul's true nature. Hence, the image of man he offers in Book ix suggests that the true human being in man is not the passions (which are instead the beast) but rather the reason. For Socrates man is fundamentally a rational being, while for Nietzsche he is fundamentally a passionate being.

Therefore, such health or strength or nobility of souls and of peoples that Nietzsche hopes to reestablish must not be based on reason but on passion. Indeed, Nietzsche suggests that the rule of reason in the soul is unhealthy. After describing the passionate self-forgetfulness of the Dionysian reveller, Nietzsche pauses to respond to the objections of those who, like Socrates, would disapprove such states of soul as sick. He finds such critics to be "poor wretches" who "have no idea how corpselike and ghostly their 'healthy-mindedness' looks when the glowing life of the Dionysian revellers roars past them." This belief that health of soul is based upon passion is also suggested in Nietzsche's claim that "Socratism" is "a sign of decline,

of weariness, of infection, of the anarchical dissolution of instincts."
A community dominated by Socratic rationalism, by dialectical inquiry, must be regarded as sick, for order or coherence in the soul
cannot be erected on reason but must rest on instinct. What is needed
is not rational contemplation of transcendent truths but passionate
affirmation of, and passionate action guided by, ideas non-rationally
held as true. In short, what we need is myth.

Music and Myth

Nietzsche presents myth as the mother of mankind—he speaks of
"the mythical maternal womb"—and suggests that her vitality is necessary for the health of her children. A myth gives coherence and
purpose to the life of a people. The mind of man is saved from "aim-
less wanderings" by myth, the images of which act as "unnoticed
omnipresent demonic guardians, under whose care the young soul
grows to maturity and whose signs help the man to interpret his life
and struggles." Myth, Nietzsche says, "wants to be experienced viv-
idly as a unique example of a universality and truth that gaze into the
infinite." Myth purports to give an account of things that is always
and everywhere true, and therefore the coherence and purpose it gives
to a people is taken to be permanent. As a result, myth enables a
people to rise above the constant change of everyday affairs and gives
a seemingly eternal significance to their lives. The pre-Socratic
Greeks had felt impelled "to relate all their experiences immediately
to their myths," and "indeed to understand them only in this relation."
Thus, for them even the "immediate present" appeared under the aspect of the eternal and "in a certain sense as timeless." And for
Nietzsche a people's nobility is directly proportional to this ability:
"any people—just as, incidentally, also any individual—is worth only
as much as it is able to press upon its experiences the stamp of the
eternal." Put another way, a people's nobility increases with the dominance of myth in its everyday life.

In contrast, a mythless people is characterized by the unhappy absence of a unified way of life, a contemptible purposelessness and slavery to the flux of the present. Contemporary society, Nietzsche claims, gives rise to "the abstract man, untutored by myth." The result is a "lawless roving of the artistic imagination, unchecked by any native myth," a "culture that has no fixed and primordial site but is doomed to exhaust all possibilities." Such a society, he continues, is given to a "frivolous deification of the present," a tendency to view all things under the aspect of the contemporary and ephemeral. That such a state of affairs is unhealthy is suggested by the ardor with which modern society seeks knowledge of older, healthy, myth-ruled cultures, as if searching desperately for a way of life ordered toward a lasting purpose. The "mythless man stands eternally hungry, surrounded by all past ages, and digs and grubs for roots, even if he has to dig for them among the remotest antiquities."

To say that cultural health depends on myth, however, is to say that it depends on Dionysian music, for myth, according to Nietzsche's account, arises from such music. He asserts "the capacity of music to give birth to *myth*" and therefore suggests that the degeneration of myth will follow the degeneration of music. He hopes that the new, Dionysian German music will lead to a rebirth of myth and therewith to a rejuvenation of German culture.

Music gives rise to myth, Nietzsche indicates, through its role in tragedy, a hybrid form of art combining a Dionysian element, the music, and an Apollinian element, the drama or story. Strictly speaking, the Apollinian element contains the myth that provides a way of life. The content of the tragic myth, Nietzsche argues, is an Apollinian event: the glorification of the fighting hero. But in glorifying the protagonist and his virtues, the myth necessarily provides an ethical teaching, that is, a presentation of a certain way of life as best.

It is, however, the Dionysian element in tragedy, the music, that impresses the myth and its ethical teaching so forcefully on the souls of the audience. For the passion of Dionysian music greatly intensifies the myth's power of attraction. By means of music "the drama attains a superlative vividness unattainable in mere spoken drama." Music does this by bringing to light "the inner world of motives," by communicating "the waves of the will" and "the swelling flood of passions" driving the action. Ultimately, such Dionysian music is culture forming because it makes the myth appear as reality, not only to a few artistically sensitive persons, but to the whole of a people. The Dionysian excitement of music, Nietzsche writes, can communicate "to a multitude" the artistic ability to see "poetic creations as real" and to be "essentially one with them."

Nietzsche views Socrates as the deadly enemy of passionate, Dionysian music and therefore holds him ultimately responsible for the degenerate state of modern society. The purposelessness of the present age is, Nietzsche contends, "the result of that Socratism which is bent on the destruction of myth." Again, music is the source of tragedy's ability to generate myth. Hence, tragedy was destroyed by the removal of Dionysian music, for without that music myth cannot blend with the poetic images and loses its persuasive force. This death of tragedy was directly the handiwork of Euripides, who sought to introduce the rule of *nous*, or intellect, into drama and who therefore had to expel the ecstatic passion of the Dionysian element. But Euripides was not the originator of this tendency. "Dionysus," Nietzsche writes, was "driven from the public stage" by "a demonic power speaking through Euripides . . . an altogether newborn demon called *Socrates*."

Confronting the Abyss

We have said that the differences between Plato's Socrates and Nietzsche over what is the most salutary music are rooted in differences about human nature. In fact they are even more deeply rooted. Ultimately their musical differences stem from different, even opposite, views of the nature of the whole and of man's relationship to it.

Here again, a superficial similarity between their teachings masks more fundamental differences. Both believe music can give expression to the nature of the cosmos. Socrates' argument in the *Republic* points to a kinship between the beautiful order of the universe and the graceful rhythm and harmony he advocates. Nietzsche is even more explicit about this kinship. He speaks of "the cosmic symbolism of music" and says that it offers a "more profound view of the world" than Apollinian art: the former leads "to the innermost heart of things" while the latter is mere "illusion."

Moreover, for both Nietzsche and Socrates, music plays a role in uniting us to the cosmos that it represents. It is connected to the philosophic experience of being one with the whole. For Socrates graceful music stimulates the immature soul's natural attraction to beautiful order and thus begins to foster an inclination toward philosophic contemplation of the orderly beauty of nature. For Nietzsche the relationship is more direct: music does not merely prepare us for philosophy but *is itself* a philosophic experience. Dionysian art—that is, music—unites us with "primordial being itself," or "with the inmost ground of the world."

Once more, these similarities are relatively superficial. For just as a gulf separates the kinds of music advocated by Socrates and Nietzsche, so it separates their understandings of the cosmos music is supposed to symbolize. The *Republic* presents the whole as characterized by rational order. The kinship Socrates posits between man and nature is actually a kinship between man's rational element and nature. For Nietzsche, however, nature or the whole is characterized by passion. He speaks of the "Dionysian basic ground of the world" and thus suggests that "the essence of nature" is "expressed symbolically" in Dionysian music. "In its intoxication," such music speaks the truth. It is "an immediate copy of the will itself," of the passionate will that is the ultimate ground of all existence. Thus the "passionately inflamed, loving, and hating man" depicted by the lyric poet-musician is in fact a "reflection of eternal being." It turns out that for Nietzsche, the satyr, the Dionysian reveller, is not only the arche-type of human nature but also "the image of nature" itself "and its strongest urges."

As Socrates' and Nietzsche's understandings of nature differ, so do their understandings of the philosophic experience of union with nature. For Socrates it is calm enjoyment of the rational order of the cosmos; for Nietzsche it is a passionate unity with a passionate uni-verse. For both, however, the human soul finds a kind of satisfaction in the philosophic experience. Just as Socrates contends that the human soul achieves happiness in such rational contemplation, so Nietzsche indicates that through music the tragic spectator experi-ences the highest pleasure. Tragic music produces a "metaphysical comfort," a sense that, in spite of the sorrowful end to which particu-lar beings must come, "life is at the bottom of things . . . indestructi-bly powerful and pleasurable." This it does by uniting the listener to "primordial being itself," the passionate will at the foundation of all things, making him feel its "raging desire for existence and joy in existence."

In this light it is tempting to claim that Nietzsche and Plato's Socrates differ on the nature of happiness. Yet this formulation would be misleading, because for Nietzsche happiness as it is understood by the ancients—a purely pleasant experience of the final satisfaction of longing—is impossible. For Nietzsche, the cosmos is in fact not a cosmos at all but a chaos. It is not, as it is for Socrates, orderly and intelligible but "contradictory" and "mysterious." Thus Nietzsche claims that the "faith" originated by Socrates, the belief that "thought" can "penetrate the deepest abysses of being," is an illusion.

As a result, the nature of the whole, both as it is in itself and as it is revealed in Dionysian music, is not that of passion moving toward final satisfaction but rather of passion simply, forever longing and forever unsatisfied. The lyric musician, Nietzsche notes, "conceives of all nature, and himself in it, as willing, as desiring, as *eternal* long-ing."[9] The Dionysian experience of oneness with the whole, then, offers, in contrast to the Socratic contemplative experience, not un-mixed pleasure but rather the mingling of pleasure and pain charac-teristic of unsatisfied desire. This experience, in which the apparent reasonable order of things is revealed to be mere illusion, is a com-bination of "blissful ecstasy" and "terror." It is blissful because the obliteration of intelligible order implies a complete emancipation of desire, which must be agreeable to a fundamentally passionate being. It is terrifying, on the other hand, because in the absence of intelli-gible order—and the end or goal it provides for passion's striving—we are condemned to the endless pain of eternally unsatisfied desire.

We can now begin to see the sense in which Nietzsche's teaching is "tragic." The passionate Dionysian experience combines pleasure and pain. We may observe, however, that the pleasure which accom-panies desire is the result of anticipated satisfaction. Yet in Nietzsche's understanding there can be no final satisfaction of desire. Ultimately, for Nietzsche, the whole, and the Dionysian experience of oneness with the whole, is characterized more fundamentally by pain or an-guish than by pleasure or joy. Thus he contends that "suffering, pri-mal and eternal," is "the sole ground of the world," that music is the "reflection of the primordial pain," and that the "Dionysian musician" is one with the primordial pain.

For Nietzsche the truth about nature and man's place in it is not, as it is for Plato's Socrates, beautiful and comforting but ugly and disturbing. Possession of this truth, which is for Socrates the very definition of human well-being, is for Nietzsche contrary to human well-being. He contends that the fruit of the Dionysian state, through which the Dionysian man has "looked in to the essence of things" and thus "*gained knowledge*," is nausea, "an ascetic, will-negating mood." He sees that "the eternal nature of things" is "out of joint." He be-comes conscious of "the absurdity of existence" and his "insight into the horrible truth" kills his capacity to act by outweighing "any mo-tive for action." The dominant element in man's nature is desire or passionate will, and therefore the activity in accord with his nature is passionate willing. But knowledge of the whole destroys his ability to desire and to act his desires by showing him that desire can never find final satisfaction—that it is vain.

If nature is so hostile to human life, if it gives man powerful longings that cannot be fulfilled, then life is not by nature worth living. Nietzsche makes this clear when he says that the Dionysian man comes to understand "the wisdom of the sylvan god, Silenus," who, according to an ancient Greek tale, revealed to King Midas that the best thing for man is "not to be born, not to *be*, to be *nothing*," and that the second best is "to die soon." The longing for life, Nietzsche holds, "does not come into being naturally and inevitably." Rather, life is made worth living only by art, by man's creation of artificial "illusions" that conceal the horrible, will-shattering truth. The Greeks, Nietzsche writes, "knew and felt the horror of existence," and in order to live they created the Apollinian world of art by which the truth could be "veiled and withdrawn from sight."

All of this raises the question: Why is Nietzsche such a proponent of tragedy? It is true that tragedy contains an Apollinian element, the drama or myth. But even that Apollinian element is in the service of the Dionysian element. Tragic drama is an Apollinian symbolic expression of the "Dionysian wisdom" conveyed more directly by the music: the ground of all being is an anguished experience of forever unsatisfied longing. Hence the "despairing cry" of Wagner's mortally wounded Tristan: "Longing! Longing! In death still longing! for very longing not dying." Tragedy points to the suffering of the hero and says, "Look closely! This is your life," teaching that "all that comes into being must be ready for a sorrowful end." But if this truth about the whole and man's place in it is so deadly, if man needs beautiful illusions in order to live, then why does Nietzsche praise tragedy so highly, the dominant element of which is the Dionysian music that so forcefully impresses the truth upon the soul?[10]

Excellence or strength of soul, with which Nietzsche is so concerned, is displayed in facing the horrible truth about nature.

Nietzsche speaks with admiration of a "pessimism of *strength*," a "predilection for the hard, gruesome, evil, problematic aspect of existence, prompted by well-being, by overflowing health, by the fulness of existence." Such a pessimism is the "sharp-eyed courage that *craves* the frightful as the . . . worthy enemy, against whom one can test one's strength." This courageous pessimism is characteristic of the culture formed by tragedy, a culture in which "wisdom . . . turns with unmoved eyes to a comprehensive view of the world, and seeks to grasp, with sympathetic feelings of love, the eternal suffering as its own." Nietzsche says forthrightly that this tragic culture is "noblest of all."

Finally, then, nobility requires more than culture, more than a life whose admirable coherence or purposefulness is the fruit of a passionate commitment to the ethical teaching of a myth. It requires in addition that such a life be accompanied by the understanding that the whole is incoherent and purposeless and therefore provides no support for or validation of the myth in light of which one lives. It requires that we imitate the hero's virtues while recognizing that nature does not reward those virtues with happiness.

This teaching seems contradictory: nobility requires that man face the truth about nature, which he cannot do without destroying himself. Hence, Nietzsche's final position appears to be that nobility requires that we face the truth to the greatest possible extent short of destroying ourselves. This we do when we experience musical tragedy, which exposes us to the Dionysian truth while simultaneously saving us from a too direct exposure to it. Nietzsche suggests that if a human being were to experience Dionysian music apart from any drama, "purely as a tremendous symphonic movement," if he were thus to "put his ear . . . to the heart chamber of the world will" and feel "the roaring desire for life" and the accompanying "innumerable shouts of pleasure and woe," he could not fail "to break suddenly." The role of the Apollinian element in tragedy, the drama or myth, is to save us from "immediate unity with Dionysian music." Next to the cosmic symbolism of music tragedy places the dramatic account of the tragic hero, who "takes the whole Dionysian world upon his back and relieves us of this burden." Tragedy exposes us to Dionysian music, but at the same time its Apollinian element distracts us from the horrifying universality and eternality of what the music represents. The Apollinian power, Nietzsche contends, restores the individual nearly shattered by music "with the healing balm of blissful illusion: suddenly we imagine that we see only . . . the hero wounded to death." The pity we feel for the particular suffering human being depicted in the drama "saves us in a way from the primordial suffering of the world" expressed in music. Tragedy, by drawing our attention to a single case of unfulfilled longing, masks to a certain extent the terrible truth expressed by its music: that all of nature is eternally unfulfilled longing.[11]

Musical tragedy, then, is an illusion. But it is the noblest of illusions insofar as it least of all shields us from the truth and hence most of all fosters that courageous pessimism which craves the horrific aspect of life as the worthy enemy. There is, Nietzsche indicates in Section 18 of *The Birth of Tragedy*, a hierarchy of illusions that human beings use to make life desirable, some more noble and others more vulgar. The various cultures are, he continues, products of the dominance in various peoples of the various illusions. But since he says elsewhere that the tragic culture is "noblest of all" cultures, we conclude that the tragic illusion is the noblest of all illusions.

We are now in a position more deeply to appreciate Nietzsche's praise of Dionysian music. Such music gives birth not just to myth, which gives rise to culture, but to tragic myth, which gives rise to the noblest culture. This is Dionysian music's most important work. The "most powerful function of music," Nietzsche states, is to invest the Homeric or Apollinian myth "with a new and most profound significance," to transform it into "a vehicle of Dionysian wisdom." And hence we are also in a position more deeply to appreciate Nietzsche's criticism of Socrates. The latter destroys not only myth but tragic myth. By banishing Dionysian music he "destroys the essence of tragedy, which can be interpreted only as a manifestation and projection into images of Dionysian states, as the visible symbolizing of music." Socrates thus destroys that by which man nobly faces the horrific truth about himself and the whole. The Socratic tendency represents a degenerate and cowardly flight from the truth, the affirmation of the "weaklings'" doctrine of "optimism."

This tendency can be seen in the *Republic*, in which Socrates wrongly, from Nietzsche's standpoint, absolutizes the Apollinian.[12] According to Nietzsche, the Apollinian plays a necessary role in human life. By its illusion of beautiful and orderly intelligibility, it heals the soul nearly shattered by the experience of Dionysian wisdom. Yet to be compatible with human nobility, which requires manfully facing the tragic nature of the whole and of human existence, the Apollinian must be experienced *as an illusion*, a contemplation of beautiful and intelligible images which are understood all along to be "*mere appearance*." The Apollinian experience becomes "pathological" if we are deceived into taking it not as mere appearance but as "crude reality." But this is precisely what takes place in the *Republic*. Socrates presents the philosophic grasping of the whole as contemplation of intelligible beauty. In Socrates' city in speech Apollinian art is used not as a relief from the ugly truth of the incoherent and passionate nature of the whole but rather as a means of leading the soul to what Nietzsche regards as a false understanding of the whole as characterized by beautiful intelligibility and order.

According to Nietzsche, this understanding of the whole gives rise to a new and degenerate "Greek cheerfulness." Unlike the older, tragic version, the new does not live resolutely in the face of the challenging truth of the incoherence of nature and the impossibility of happiness. Rather it blissfully embraces life as a result of its comforting but false belief that nature is orderly and happiness is possible. Socratic rationalism is essentially optimistic and therefore necessarily incompatible with tragedy. It holds that existence is comprehensible, that thought "can penetrate the deepest abysses of being" and fathom the nature of things. This belief is accompanied by the conviction that knowledge is a panacea, that knowledge is virtue, and that the virtuous man is happy. In sum, Socratic rationalism, unlike tragic Nietzscheanism, holds that the whole is intelligible and that man can achieve happiness by grasping and living in accordance with its order.

This understanding of things, hostile to tragedy in principle, actually found its way into Greek drama and destroyed tragedy in practice. The philosopher instructed the playwright, and Euripides became "the poet of aesthetic Socratism." He removed the Dionysian element and reconstructed tragedy "purely on the basis of an un-Dionysian," which is to say untragic, "world-view." He expelled music, the expression of the blind longing of nature, and in its place introduced *nous*, intelligibility. But since the dramatic depiction of the suffering of the hero arises from music's expression of the suffering of nature, and since intelligibility is necessarily accompanied by optimism, passionate music's replacement by *nous* results in a radically different kind of story. The Socratic-Euripidean drama offers "an earthly resolution of the tragic dissonance" by which the hero's virtue is, after some hardship, rewarded by happiness in the form of "a splendid marriage or tokens of divine favor." Thanks to Socrates, the profundity of musical oneness with nature's suffering was replaced by the mendacity of the happy ending, and that art by which man developed his strength was perverted into one which is both a sign and cause of his weakness.

Music and Passion

T HE TEACHING ABOUT MUSIC in the work of the thinkers we
have explored is problematic in two ways. In the first place,
this teaching is not self-evidently true. The musical political
philosophers agree that music has a natural and politically relevant
power to affect our feelings and hence to shape our actions. Indeed,
this cornerstone of the arguments of the ancients and the later
moderns is acknowledged, specifically in Montesquieu's *The Spirit of
the Laws*, even by the early moderns who choose to dispense with
music in favor of what they regard as more reliable ways of influencing
human behavior. Yet one could reasonably question whether music
in fact possesses such power.

Second, in a sense the history of political philosophy itself offers
no coherent teaching on the relationship of music to politics. The
thinkers who have addressed this issue, while agreeing on music's
power and political significance, disagree on what to do about it.
Should we ignore it, as the early moderns suggest, use it to calm passion and awaken reason, as Plato and Aristotle recommend, or following Rousseau and Nietzsche, use it to excite passion and silence
reason? Here the history of political philosophy does not so much
offer us a teaching as it confronts us with a question: To which ac-

count of politics, music, and human nature should we turn to bring clarity and wisdom to current controversies about pop music?

Music and Nature

All of the political philosophers who have taken music seriously as a political force insist on its natural status. Musical activity, and hence its power over the human soul, they contend, is something proper to human nature and not a merely conventional or cultural phenomenon. Thus the *Republic* speaks of the "charm" that "meter, rhythm, and harmony . . . by nature possess," and Aristotle finds that we have "a natural instinct" for "harmony and rhythm." Rousseau indicates that culture itself, in the form of the earliest human communities, could only come into being through the prior existence of melody's natural ability to unite human beings in common passions of the heart. Similarly, Nietzsche suggests that Dionysian music both arises from and can touch the depths of man's fundamentally passionate nature. Indeed, his hope that it can revitalize a decadent culture indicates that for Nietzsche music must be rooted in something more profound than culture.

The credibility of these claims of music's natural status is central to the argument of this book. If music, its power over the soul, and its consequent social and political impact are all dependent entirely on culture, then we can learn nothing useful about these matters from cultures different from our own. Generally speaking, if human life is entirely or overwhelmingly the product of culture, if there is no such thing as human nature, then political philosophy, understood as the attempt to discover truths about human beings as such, truths that transcend the particularities of time and place, is impossible. More specifically, if music and its relationship to political life are utterly dependent on culture, then there is no culture-transcending wisdom about these matters, and efforts to gain practical insight from the history of political philosophy is bound to be fruitless.

We cannot, moreover, dispense with this issue by positing music's rootedness in nature as a fact so obvious as to require no supporting argument. On the contrary, the modern mind is powerfully influenced by an understanding of nature that tends to deny music a natural status. Under the twin tutelage of modern political philosophy and Darwinian biological science, many of us reflexively think of only those things pertaining to our perpetuation, either individually or as a species, as natural. Yet the survival value of music is far from obvious, and on the utilitarian and Darwinian understanding music seems to be merely a cultural "extra." One scientist notes that because "music is sought as entertainment," which is "certainly not necessary for life," the "standard treatment of music" tends to regard it merely as "the product of culture."[1] What evidence, then, can persuade us, contrary to our first inclination, that music is natural? We might in the first place turn to the principle of universality. Activities "closely linked to biology" or nature, the same scientist notes, "should be universal" and manifest themselves "across different cultures."[2]

A preliminary point in favor of the universality of music is the very history of political philosophy explored in the previous chapters. That history shows, if nothing else, that music and the belief in its power to move the soul in politically relevant ways are not just the eccentric peculiarity of one culture alone. Plato and Aristotle, reflecting on the radically politicized societies of ancient Greece, and Rousseau and Nietzsche, taking as the beginning of their investigations the modern bourgeois societies of Europe, alike bear witness to music's importance. These thinkers, moreover, are not alone in attributing to music a natural status and a natural power to move the passions. Such notions are found not only at the beginning of Western philosophy and in its more recent stages but also in the long intervening tradition of thought of the Christian moralists and philosophers. Thus our natural affinity for music is affirmed by such intellectual luminaries as St. John Chrysostom, Boethius, Isidore of Seville, St. Basil, and St. Augustine of Hippo.[3]

One might respond that even the common testimony of all these authors can still be interpreted as somewhat parochial and thus inconclusive with regard to the universality of music. That testimony, after all, comes exclusively from thinkers commonly regarded as representatives of the "Western tradition" or "Western civilization." Yet the very fact that we use such terms suggests some kind of cultural continuity running all the way from Socrates to Nietzsche. This argument would hold that the power of music observed by these thinkers is very likely merely a cultural phenomenon, since all were looking at fundamentally the same culture.

In response to this objection one might point to the teaching on music and character found in Confucianism, though the evidence of only one non-Western culture would no doubt be deemed insufficient to demonstrate music's universality. Happily, however, solid evidence of this universality can be found in the researches of contemporary anthropology and ethnomusicology. Scholars in these fields find music to be "omnipresent," a "universal practice." In the words of one scientist: "you can't find a culture that doesn't have music."[4]

Furthermore, this apparent universality of music is no mere façade: "music" is not an empty term covering such a wide variety of phenomena that in practice it describes no universally constant activity. On the contrary, contemporary research reveals that music possesses universal characteristics that mark it as a similar behavior present in all human societies. For example, the principle of "octave equivalence"—the treatment of two pitches, one with a frequency twice that of the other, as the same pitch sounding at different octaves—is "present in all the world's music systems," and it is typical across cultures to organize scales around the consonant intervals of octaves, fifths, and fourths.[5] The findings of ethnology even reveal striking similarities in the music sung to babies in a wide variety of cultures. Lullabies universally "tend to have smooth descending contours, slow tempo, relatively simple structure, and repetition."[6] At this point one cannot help but notice the similarity between the "simple" rhythm and harmony advocated in the *Republic* as a means to still the passions of the young, on the one hand, and the music apparently typically used to calm infants in a variety of cultures, on the other.

The presence of music in a diversity of cultures, while suggestive, does not, however, fully demonstrate its naturalness. As one scientist warns, the universality of a phenomenon "is a necessary rather than a sufficient criterion" by which to establish its natural status.[7] A universally observed phenomenon might, after all, result not from nature but from some ancient common cultural origins for all contemporary societies or the successful dispersion of cultural practices from one society to others. We must, then, ask what further evidence could strengthen the case for the naturalness of music.

It is common to associate innate behaviors with nature and learned behaviors with culture. Therefore, if responsiveness to music is found to be somehow internal to human beings rather than external, something that is present in us from the beginning rather than something we pick up later and only through repeated efforts at assimilation, this would be evidence of the naturalness of music.

Here again, the fruits of contemporary social and biological science lend support to the contention of the political philosophers that music exists by nature. Recent studies indicate that, like "language and speech, musical behavior also appears early in life, is spontaneous rather than merely imitative, and is integrated into child play without adult supervision or demands."[8] Controlled observations of infants listening to music suggest that they can discern differences in pitch smaller than a semitone, the smallest interval used in Western music, and that they "perceive and remember melodic contour"—that is, like adults they recognize melodies not by attending to the exact pitches but rather to the relationships among them, to the organization of the tune—as well as "recognize melodies independently of tempo" and "detect changes in rhythm."[9] There is even evidence that newborns recognize themes to which they had been exposed before birth.[10] Other research indicates that babies as little as four months

old not only discern the difference between consonance and dissonance but also prefer the former to the latter.[11] And infants less than
six months old have been found to prefer "Mozart minuets that have
short pauses inserted between phrases"—that is, between passages
representing distinct musical statements—to versions of the same
pieces in which the musical organization is disrupted by inserting
pauses in the middle of phrases.[12]

Here one cannot help but remark, once again, the striking similarities between the ancient account of music and the discoveries of
modern science. The ancients teach that the human soul possesses
by nature an attraction to rationally discernible order and that orderly
music is by nature capable of addressing that attraction even when
the soul is at its earliest stages of development. Yet contemporary
research seems to suggest much the same thing when it reveals that
children—infants so young that the influence of culture on their
minds must be judged minimal if not nonexistent—not only perceive
but also prefer, not just the fundamental organizational structures of
music such as rhythm and harmony but also the larger musical order found in melodic phrases.

Music and Passion

The political philosophers we have examined assert not only that
music is natural but also that it is, or at least that the right kind of
music can be, a form of communication that imitates the passions and
arouses them in the listener. Here again, however, their claims are
subject to doubt. Some might, while admitting its natural status,
contend that music, rather than being a language of the feelings, is a
purely intellectual affair, a system of abstract symbols that refers to
nothing beyond itself.

In response we can point to the opinion held down through the
ages by musicians themselves that their art is a means of expressing
and inspiring the passions. We first find this belief expressed by the

music theorists of Plato and Aristotle's time. M. L. West, in his *Ancient Greek Music*, reports that various rhythms were commonly thought to imitate particular passions and to induce a similar state of soul in the listeners. Thus, for example, the predominance of long over short notes in a piece "was held to conduce to a calm and serious (but not quiescent) state of mind." Similarly, in the literature of the time one also finds the "emotional qualities" of mode "and their effect on the disposition of the listener" treated as "of the greatest interest and importance."[13]

The leading figures of the musical tradition with which Rousseau and Nietzsche were familiar also affirmed the ability of music to inspire the passions. The early composer of opera, Giulio Caccini, wrote that "the musician's end" is to "delight and move the affections of the mind." In a similar vein, the famous composer Claudio Monteverdi, writing in 1638, contended that the "purpose which all good music should have" is "greatly" to "move our mind." And Leopold Mozart, the famous father of the still more famous son, castigated those performers "who have no conception whatever of the passion that is supposed to be expressed in" the compositions they butcher.[14]

This understanding of music runs consistently through the writings of many of the great composers of the nineteenth century. Weber, for instance, spoke of music as "the purest, most ethereal language of the passions" and of the musician as a "powerful master of every passionate stimulus," able to "draw our affections" into a world in which he "causes us with him and through him to feel pain, pleasure, horror, joy, hope, and love." Liszt contended that music communicates "our affections . . . directly in their full intensity" and thus "permeates" our senses "like a dart, like a ray, like a dew, like a spirit, and fills our soul." He even asserted for "instrumental music" alone the power to "give to certain feelings and passions an expression intelligible to the listener," thereby "affecting his soul."[15]

The evidence of contemporary science tends to confirm the opinion that music is able to move the passions. One team of researchers, for example, found that "patients receiving 12 weeks of daily music therapy" in the form of exposure to Mozart and Mendelssohn "were less depressed and anxious, and more stable and sociable, than other patients in the same facility."[16] Another study revealed that 90 percent of the subjects examined claimed that the music to which they were exposed provoked physical reactions typical of various kinds of specific emotional arousal, such as tears, laughter, and the experiencing of a shiver down the back or of a lump in the throat.[17] Similarly, on the basis of a review of the empirical studies of music's emotional impact, one scholar was able to formulate a series of

> generalizations about the musical qualities that induce different moods. Excitement is produced by music in the major mode, that is fast, of medium pitch, uneven rhythm, dissonant harmony, and loud volume. Tranquility is produced by music in the major mode, slow tempo, medium pitch, flowing rhythm, consonant harmony, and soft volume. Happiness is induced by the major mode, fast tempo, high pitch, flowing rhythm, consonant harmony, and medium volume. Serious music is in a major mode with low pitch, firm rhythm, consonant harmony, and medium volume. Sadness is produced by the minor mode, slow tempo, low pitch, firm rhythm, and dissonant harmony.[18]

At this point doubters could respond that music's supposed ability to move the passions, even if it does exist, might be merely a Western phenomenon. After all, the composers and theorists to whom we have referred are all, once again, members of the Western tradition of music, and much of scientific evidence arises from studies involving Americans or Europeans. Once more, however, the testimony of social science that looks beyond the West suggests otherwise. David Hargreaves and Adrian North, in the introduction to their *The Social Psychology of Music*, suggest that music's affective power is rooted in nature rather than convention when they claim, in the context of affirming its transcultural communicative power, that music "can arouse deep and profound emotions within us" and that such feelings "can be shared experiences between people from quite different backgrounds."[19]

Anthropologists similarly find in non-Western cultures the use of music to imitate and move the passions. John Kaemmer, for example, in *Music in Human Life: Anthropological Perspectives on Music*, writes of men in New Guinea "driven to weeping by the beauty of the singing of the women."[20] Similarly, Alan Merriam, in his classic study *The Anthropology of Music*, claims that "there is considerable evidence to indicate that music functions widely and on a number of levels as a means of emotional expression."[21] As an example, he reviews a study of one tribal people finding that "stimulating and expressing emotion in the performers" and "imparting it to the listeners" is one of the functions of their music.[22] In fact, Kaemmer even admits that music's affective power may be rooted at least in part in human nature. Thus he writes that "although many of the affective qualities" of music "are based on culturally determined values," it is nonetheless "possible that some affective reactions result from the operation of universal human cognitive and affective processes."[23]

Further evidence of the emotional power of music as a transcultural phenomenon can be found in Gilbert Rouget's cross-cultural study of the extraordinary state he calls trance or possession:

> Of all the arts, music is undoubtedly the one that has the greatest capacity to move us, and the emotion it arouses can reach overwhelming proportions. Since trance is clearly an emotional form of behavior, it is not surprising that musical emotions should prove to be destined, to some extent, to become institutionalized in this form. This would mean that we are dealing here with a relationship between music and trance that, although strongly influenced by culture, is nevertheless based on a natural—and thus universal—property of music, or at least of a certain kind of music. Moreover, in emotional trance it is music alone that produces the trance."[24]

Rouget later gives evidence supporting Kaemmer's suspicion that some emotional reactions to music may be based in nature, noting that the rhythms of trance-inducing music have two frequently recurring characteristics across cultures: "on the one hand breaks or abrupt changes of rhythm, on the other an accelerando crescendo, which recurs so frequently that one might view it as a universal of possession music."[25]

Music and Politics

We come, then, to the claim that is the most important point of agreement among Plato, Aristotle, Rousseau, and Nietzsche and at the same time probably the most controversial aspect of their teaching on music. They contend not only that music arouses in the listener the passions depicted but that it can move the passions powerfully enough to influence our thoughts and actions. Their insistence on music's political importance rests on this belief. Music, for these political philosophers, is far from being merely a diversion that engages our feelings sufficiently to entertain but not enough to move us to action. On the contrary, they all affirm that music's grip on the soul can be potent enough to shape an entire people's way of life.

Traditional common opinion lends support to such claims. Most of us are aware of the cliché holding that "music hath charms to soothe the savage breast," and we dimly recall the Old Testament's account of David's calming of King Saul through his playing on the lyre. Such things have been said in many cultures down through the centuries. A Japanese myth tells of a musician who, upon finding that his house had been robbed, began playing his flute. According to the story, "the music was so beautiful that the burglar, upon hearing it, stopped fleeing, returned with the stolen goods, and asked forgiveness."[26] The Greeks told a similar tale of Pythagoras calming a young man on the brink of rash action by "persuading the piper to play a

more dignified melody."[27] Nor has an appreciation of the direct political implications of music's power over the soul been utterly absent
from such stories. Another Greek tale claims that when Sparta was
in a state of civil turmoil, an oracle advised calling in the singer
Terpander, whose music, so goes the story, swiftly "restored the city
to good order."[28] As one anthropologist notes, stories such as these
may or may not have some grounding in fact, but they certainly do
suggest "the kind of power attributed to music" in the wide variety
of cultures in which they appear.[29]

Of course, even if such a belief in music's potency is widespread
it does not necessarily follow that it is true. We might, like one recent writer skeptical of music's ability to influence action, concede the
prevalence of such stories and nevertheless dismiss them as a kind
of popular delusion.[30] On the other hand, when investigating matters
accessible to ordinary human experience it is more sensible to follow Aristotle and defer to a certain extent to common opinion, taking it at least as a reasonable starting point in the quest for wisdom.

But Aristotle would not have us simply rest satisfied with common opinion, and fortunately we need not do so, for contemporary
science tends to confirm the belief that music can influence behavior.
Some of the evidence here has been generated by the burgeoning field
of music therapy and therefore speaks to the impact of music on the
mentally or emotionally disturbed. In one case some researchers
found that music reduced the aggressive behavior of psychiatric patients, and a similar study revealed that music piped into the dining
room resulted in calmer and more cooperative behavior on the part
of patients suffering from dementia.[31] Such research also testifies to
music's capacity to provoke a very different result. Another study
reported "a significantly higher frequency of aggressive and difficult
behavior when 'hard rock' and 'rap' background music was played
than when 'easy listening' and 'country' music was played" for the
patients in a mental health hospital.[32]

Music appears to be no less able to influence the behavior of people who do not suffer from mental and emotional disorders. One experiment in psychology supports the political philosophers' belief in the ability of music to enhance the persuasiveness of speech. It revealed that musical presentations of various social and political issues resulted in more movement of attitudes among the subjects than nonmusical presentations on the same topics.[33] Another study indicates the ability of a certain kind of music to influence behavior by intensifing feelings of aggression. In this experiment, subjects were insulted by a person who was, unbeknownst to them, an assistant to the researcher conducting the study. The subjects then were given an opportunity to wreak vengeance on their antagonist by administering a relatively weak electric shock and were exposed to various kinds of music while they determined their course of action. The result: people who were exposed to loud and complex music were more likely to punish their tormenters. In light of such evidence one scholar concludes that "affect induced by music has significant implications for social behavior."[34] With regard to music's ability to shape human action, the findings of contemporary social science harmonize well with the claims of Plato, Aristotle, Rousseau, and Nietzsche.

Furthermore, in the light of such findings it is surely not extravagant to conclude that music is politically important. After all, if music can influence behavior in individuals and small groups, it seems likely that it can do so on a large enough scale to be of political relevance. In any case, on this point we need not rely on extrapolations from the evidence already mentioned but can find confirmation of music's political salience in the testimony of the modern investigation of human cultures. One anthropologist and ethnomusicologist reports that "ethnography has revealed that in diverse times and climes" the organization of political life "may be supported by or even unworkable without musical performance." For two examples he points to Africa, where in the southern Sudan the Nuer selected as their captain in war the "most inspiring singer of martial anthems" and in

South Africa the indigenous people cannot "engage in civil protest without the performance of 'menacing' songs and dances."[35]

Similar support for the political importance of music is provided by anthropologist John Kaemmer, who observes that "because music has considerable power to mobilize the sentiment and action of masses of people, it becomes an important political tool," as, for example, when songs serve "to mobilize sentiment in favor of war."[36] In particular he points to music's role, through its capacity for "enhancing communication" and imparting a sense of shared feeling among people, in "building and maintaining group identity" and strengthening commitment to that identity.[37] Thus, for example, the music of the Tuareg, dwellers of the Saharan desert, "symbolizes the noblest ideals and sentiments" of their culture and is used by them to "inspir[e] men to heroic deeds" and "to give courage to warriors in times of battle."[38]

Here one cannot help but notice the conspicuous similarity between, on the one hand, what contemporary anthropology regards as the political function of music in many cultures and, on the other, the purposes for which the musical political philosophers recommend the power of music be used. For both, it seems, find in music a potent device for binding individuals into a larger community of thought, feeling, and action. In the *Republic* Socrates famously posits unity as the greatest good for the city, and rhythm and harmony, as we have seen, play a crucial role in supporting that unity through the common education they provide in the noble and the beautiful. Similarly, Aristotle holds that a shared understanding of the good and the bad is necessary for the city's well-being, and his best regime makes use of music education to impart that common ethic. Again, Rousseau's music seeks to inspire passionate commitment to the laws and the community, and Nietzsche speaks of music's role in impressing on the soul of a people the myth at the heart of their culture.

Kaemmer also indicates that while music can strengthen group identity it can as easily be a source of social disintegration. Among its other social functions, he contends, music is frequently found to legitimize activities typically forbidden. Hence the peril that it may "legitimize forms of behavior that are socially disruptive."[39]

> People in Western society are blissfully unaware of some of the basic functions of music. The propagation of profitable forms of music has contributed to the perception that music is merely a form of entertainment. As a result, many people engage in musical behavior without considering the real functions of music. Function in this sense refers to the consequences of musical experience, whether they are intentional or not. Many of these functions are operating even when the music is viewed primarily as entertainment, and the functions can be either negative or positive. One of these functions is to legitimize other areas of activity, and this can have a negative effect when popular music appears to legitimize the use of drugs, violence as a solution to problems, and a view of women as sex objects.[40]

The similarity to the teaching of Book IV of the *Republic* is striking. Socrates warns that the guardians must take special care to supervise the "ways of music" in the city in speech because those ways are never changed without leading to wholesale alterations in the very character of the regime. Yet, Socrates observes, the invasion of lawlessness through music usually occurs unknown to the city and its rulers, since most mistakenly view music as nothing more than "a kind of play" that can "do no harm."[41] It seems that, with regard to the political importance of music, the wisdom of the musical political philosophers and the insights of contemporary anthropology are substantially the same.

Character and Mind

It is also necessary to evaluate the plausibility of two claims about the power of music that are associated particularly with the ancient political philosophers: that music has a permanent impact on both character and mind, that it can, at least when it plays a prominent role in the lives of the young, leave a lasting impression on the soul. In light of the preceding observations, to reject music's power to form character would seem more the result of willful denial than of honest doubt. As we have seen not only from the political philosophers we have studied but also from the most recent social science, music moves the passions and moves them powerfully enough to influence action. But what is character but a settled disposition to feel and act in certain ways? If, as Aristotle teaches and as few would deny, character results from habit, from repeatedly acting and feeling in certain ways, then surely sufficient exposure to a certain kind of music, along with the feelings it inspires and actions it encourages, can form one's character.

Indeed, the relationship between music and character accords well with common sense, as historian Paul Rahe nicely illustrates by thinking through the classical teaching using music familiar to the modern reader. "To us," he observes, "the claims initially advanced on music's behalf [by numerous ancient authors] may well seem bizarre." "And yet," he continues, "when one pauses to think about the question, it is not difficult to see how a young man nurtured exclusively on Bach would be likely to develop tastes, habits, and a general disposition distinguishing him from a counterpart similarly reared on John Philip Sousa. Nor, to take an even more striking example, is it hard to see how the former and the latter would differ from a comparable young man subjected to a steady diet of rock and roll."[42] We could profitably ask ourselves if we would prefer that the future spouses of our children nurture their souls on Vivaldi or Marilyn Manson. Any honest consideration of such hypotheticals reveals that our unreflective opinions, unenlightened by the conclusions of political philosophy, support the idea that music and character are inextricably intertwined.

The argument for music's power to form character appears even stronger when we consider the ancient emphasis on the impressionability of the young. If the immature soul is ready to receive the stamp that anyone happens to place on it, as Plato's Socrates says and as Aristotle agrees, then it would seem to follow that music's power to move the soul must be respected all the more when applied to those human beings who are at their most malleable stage. Moreover, the plausibility of such concerns is supported by recent science that indicates the remarkable plasticity of the still developing human brain.[43] As it turns out, the mature state of the brain is not completely predetermined by inborn genetic information but is instead influenced to a considerable degree by the stimulation the organ experiences as it develops. This revelation has important implications for our understanding of the development of the intellect, an issue to which we will return presently. But, as the brain is the physical seat not only of our cognitive capacities but also of the emotions, the plasticity of the brain possesses no less important implications for the development of character. It appears that early experiences can have a lasting impact on the elements of the brain that process feelings, such that certain emotional habits, which make up what we call character, emerge.[44]

What, then, of Plato and Aristotle's claim that music can engage and develop the reason? One could very easily be tempted to let this, surely one of the more outlandish of the classical notions about music, pass unremarked. Yet to do so would seem impossible, given the important role this notion evidently plays in Plato's and Aristotle's thought. As we have seen, both teach that the right education in rhythm and harmony can prepare the soul for philosophic activity. Moreover, it does this not only by calming the passions, thereby allowing reason an opportunity to speak and be heard in the soul, but also by actively engaging reason itself, awakening and cultivating its natural love of rationally discernible order. Indeed, it may be that in some sense the graceful and orderly music of Plato and Aristotle calms the passions by awakening the reason, insofar as the activity of one part of the soul tends to impede that of another.

Turning a final time to the evidence of contemporary science, we do find support for this classical notion. Although there appear to be specific areas of the brain dedicated to the processing of musical information, much research indicates nonetheless that musical experience activates not only such regions but also others that are more commonly associated with other kinds of intellectual activity. Some of this evidence comes from observation of those who have suffered some damage to the brain. For example, one scholar states that "there is some evidence . . . that brain lesions . . . which interfere with grammatical constructions of spoken language also interfere with the ordering of any but the simplest melodic structures in music."[45] Similarly, another researcher reports that in the clinical literature it is common to find that both music and language skills are disrupted when the left hemisphere of the brain is damaged. From this he concludes that "the brain areas responsible for music seem to have a partial, but incomplete, overlap with those responsible for language."[46]

The newly possible use of technology to investigate undamaged brain tissue lends support to such conclusions. The research of one brain scientist finds that exposure to different patterns of pitches activates an area of the brain associated with the processing of visual images and that listening to musical excerpts activates a region of the left brain associated with our capacity for spoken language.[47] Says one neuropsychologist: "I have very little doubt that when you are listening to a real piece of music, you are engaging the entire brain."[48]

In the light of such evidence it is not surprising to find a number of recent studies pointing to music's ability to enhance the capacity of the mind in areas distinct from music itself. One survey of the scientific literature on music reports a study showing that music training caused first grade students to do better in reading than their un-

trained colleagues.[49] Other researchers, noting the similarities between the appreciation of music and spatial temporal reasoning—
both involve "the ability to create, maintain, transform, and relate
complex mental images even in the absence of external sensory in-
put or feedback"—have investigated the possibility that music might
act as a kind of "pre-language" that can enhance one's ability to per-
form such abstract reasoning.[50] The most publicized experiment
along these lines was conducted by Frances Rauscher and her colleagues at the University of California, Irvine, who found that listening to Mozart enhanced student performance on a test of spatial
reasoning.[51] In this case the effect of music on ability was found to
be temporary, but a later study by the same team found that after four
months of music training preschoolers displayed more lasting improvements in their spatial intelligence, leading Rauscher to specu-
late that the improvements could be permanent.[52]

Indeed, given the findings regarding the plasticity of the developing brain, it would be more surprising to find that such early exposure to music, or at least some kind of music, does not have lasting
benefits for the mind. The connections in the brain required for high
level thinking do not simply grow spontaneously but are rather
formed by activity, by stimulation of the brain as it develops. One
study found that a certain part of the brain linking the two hemispheres was substantially more developed in musicians who had
trained from an early age than in non-musicians.[53] It seems, then,
that the ancient claims about a certain music's friendliness to reason
find support in modern science no less than their claims about
music's ability to move the passions.

The Musical Controversy in Political Philosophy

Establishing the credibility of the political philosophers' common
assertions of music's power over the soul, however, does not of itself

provide us with a teaching in light of which we can resolve our disputes over pop music, for these thinkers still disagree on how best to use music's power. We cannot simply ask political philosophy to address our current controversies, because political philosophy is itself characterized by controversy on the most fundamental questions, which up to this point we have described in the following way: For the ancients music is crucial because, properly used, it can still the passions and awaken the reason, thus serving the city and preparing the individual for the happiness of virtuous action and philosophic contemplation. The early moderns, in contrast, convinced of the natural dominance of passion in human nature, disregard music as a political and educational tool, choosing instead to erect the polity on an appeal to untutored passion, and in particular to the desire for life and comfort. Rousseau and Nietzsche, appalled at the baseness of the modern project, resurrect the political concern with music, using it to inflame the passions in the service of a new politics of nobility.

This way of framing the controversy, however, is problematic, for it uses the term "passion," and presents the role of passion in this history of thought, in a way that is too simplistic. We have said, more or less, that the ancients are the enemies of passion and the moderns, both early and late, its friend. This simplicity has, up to this point, been useful, as it has served to highlight the great divide between the ancient elevation of reason and the modern emphasis on desire or feeling. Nevertheless, this presentation, whatever clarity it achieves in some respects, tends to obscure certain important aspects of music's place in the history of political philosophy.

Consider, in the first place, the difficulty involved in saying that the ancients seek to use the charms of music to calm passion and awaken reason. This difficulty comes to light when we reflect that on Plato's and Aristotle's account music achieves these goals by cultivating reason's natural *longing* for order. As the use of the word "longing" suggests, reason itself is not devoid of desire, and in this sense the ancient teaching, no less that the early and late modern teachings, bases politics on a kind of passion.[54]

Consider further the problem that arises from saying that the early moderns build on untutored passion while their late modern successors build on passion intensified by passionate music. Such a formulation fails fully to convey the difference between the two camps, for in saying that both build on "passion" it seems to say that both build on the same thing. But this cannot be the case. After all, Rousseau and Nietzsche recoil in disgust from what they take to be the low concerns around which Hobbes, Locke, and Montesquieu seek to organize political life. This implies that the former place at the center of their politics a passion different from the one upon which their early modern predecessors sought to found society. Indeed, the distance between the two approaches appears clearly in the contrast between, on the one hand, the early modern emphasis on the desires for life and comfort, which arise from the body, and, on the other, Rousseau's celebration of the language arising from the "passions of the heart" and his related denigration of that based on the needs of the body.

We need, then, to reformulate our account of the musical controversy in political philosophy. Perhaps such a reformulation can be devised on the basis of the *Republic*'s teaching on the soul. In Book IV Socrates and his companions come to an understanding of the soul as made up of three distinct elements: the rational part, which calculates; the spirited part, by which we can become angry; and the desiring part, by which we feel pleasure. In Book IX, however, Socrates returns to the nature of the soul and offers a modification of his earlier teaching. He referred to the "desiring" part, he says, only as a kind of shorthand, because that part of the soul deals with the desires and pleasures that are most obvious and intense, those of the body. But the other parts of the soul, as it turns out, also have certain desires. The spirited part desires and takes pleasure in honor or glory, while the rational part finds satisfaction in knowledge or wisdom, the contemplation of eternally unchanging truths.

In this light we can offer the following modified summation of this controversy. The ancients use music to calm the bodily and spirited desires and to cultivate rational desire, believing as they do that reason or intellect, though perhaps the smallest part of man, is nonetheless his true self and, therefore, that in the satisfaction of its longings the whole soul ultimately finds its happiness.

The early moderns, in contrast, doubt the existence of reason as the ancients understand it and the reality of the things to which the ancients contend it is attracted. That is, they do not take seriously the notion of reason as a part of man that shares in the nature of, and is drawn to contemplation of, the eternal order of the cosmos. If such things exist, they are politically irrelevant, given the sheer power of bodily desire and its inevitable triumph in the souls of most men most of the time. Seeking to erect political society on this more stable foundation, the moderns dispense with music. After all, the passions for security and comfort, being the dominant elements of our nature, need no assistance from music's charm.

Rousseau and Nietzsche, appalled at the lowness of a politics in the service of mere bodily desire, seek once again to establish nobility or excellence as the end of social life. Like their modern predecessors, however, they are dismissive of the ancient notion of reason as the core of human nature. Therefore their return to nobility must be accomplished on the basis of something else in man. Hence their use of music to cultivate the spirited desires. In Book ix of the *Republic* Socrates offers an "image" of man: in each one of us there dwells a human being, representing reason, a lion, representing spiritedness, and a many-headed beast, representing the desires of the body. Rousseau and Nietzsche say, in effect: It is base to take one's bearings from the beast, and we know that the human being is a fantasy, but it is still possible to live as the lion. But, thanks to the efforts of the philosophers of "political hedonism,"[55] modern man is sunk so deep in the bestial that the only way to reawaken the lion is through the roar of a passionate music that can drown out the voice of the petty, narrow, calculating reason that now serves man's animal appetites while holding in check his more honorable spirited desires.

One might take issue with this equation of Platonic spiritedness with the "passion" of Rousseau and Nietzsche, but it is clear that there is a substantial similarity. In the *Republic* Socrates links spiritedness with the desire for honor and victory. Yet this thirst for the distinction accompanying rule over others seems to have animated the regimes that awakened the warmest admiration in Rousseau, Sparta and Rome, as well as the men that Nietzsche found the best, Julius Caesar and Napoleon. Moreover, in classical political philosophy spiritedness, or *thumos*, is characterized by more than just the love of glory. It is also the basis of the love of one's own, our capacity for commitment to the way of life of our community. The spirited guardians of the *Republic*'s city in speech remind Socrates of noble dogs who are gentle with those they know and savage with those they do not. Aristotle says that spiritedness is the part of us by which we feel affection for others, which he elsewhere indicates is the glue that holds the city together. Again, the teaching of Rousseau and Nietzsche seems to stress the musical stimulation of spiritedness thus understood. Both make music the instrument by which to excite in men a passionate attachment to the way of life of the community, to the laws of the city in Rousseau's thought and to the myth at the heart of the culture in Nietzsche's.

Choosing a Guide

Our awareness of these competing visions of the proper relationship of music to politics prompts us to wonder, and to try to judge, which one among them comes closest to capturing the truth. To put it bluntly, who is right? The musical or the amusical political philosophers? If the former, the musical moderns, Rousseau and Nietzsche, or the musical ancients, Plato and Aristotle?

This task of judging among the alternatives is unavoidable because it is necessary to bring some coherence to the contemporary disputes surrounding the influence of popular music on the young. The parties to the current argument operate on different understandings of how important music is to our public life and disagree as to what should be considered a healthy musical influence. Yet these are essentially the same questions that divide the political philosophers we have examined. Hence, we cannot simply turn to the history of political philosophy for an easy solution to the arguments we find raging in our own day. We must choose a philosophical guide from among the thinkers we have encountered if we are to come away from this history with some consistent set of principles to apply to our own controversies.

To begin with, a case can be made against the amusical politics of the early moderns. It is undeniable that modern liberal regimes have had tremendous success in providing security and prosperity for their citizens. Nevertheless, few of even their most ardent proponents would dare to assert that the political life of such regimes is noble or beautiful. It is harsh, but by no means unfair, to say with Richard Hooker that modern politics is guided by the uninspiring belief that government is ordained "for no other ende and purpose but only to fatt up men like hogges and see that they have their mash."[56] Since men are not hogs and are capable of more than merely enjoying their mash, such a politics seems to fail to fully satisfy the longings of our nature.

To advance this criticism, however, is to find fault with our own regime, which is indirectly the fruit of early modern political philosophy. Taking instruction from Hobbes, Locke, Montesquieu, and other thinkers of a similar cast of mind, the American founders thought self-interested passion a more potent force in human nature than virtue- and wisdom-loving reason. Therefore, they sought to establish not a government that would promote human excellence but one that would provide security and comfort.[57] Holding that "moral" motives are insufficient to restrain fractious passions, they turned away from character formation as a means even to the lowered goals of the government they were founding.[58] Instead, they sought to protect the individual's life and property by means of various institutional arrangements—such as the "regular distribution of power into distinct departments," the "introduction of legislative balances and checks," the "institution of courts composed of judges, holding their offices during good behavior," the "representation of the people in the legislature by deputies of their own election," and the "enlargement" of the size of the country—which they hoped would, by using passion to restrain passion, make up for the "defect" of the "better motives" they despaired of inculcating.[59]

Here, incidentally, we find the probable cause of contemporary political science's indifference to the questions of music and character mentioned in the introduction. In a regime founded on the early modern theory of politics, there is a strong presumption against according a public place to such concerns. Yet contemporary political science's account of politics arises largely from observation of contemporary political practice. Thus its understanding of politics is captive of the regime's ideology, and its posture toward music is distinctly modern. Following Hobbes and his successors in viewing man as motivated primarily by material factors and in therefore understanding politics as primarily geared toward providing for man's bodily needs, political science tends to neglect those concerns, such as refinement of character and of mind, that open the door to music's political relevance. Professing to be a science, to seek universal knowledge of political life, it is in fact blinded by prejudice, by an uncritical acceptance of conventional wisdom, to an account of politics according to which music cannot be politically important.

There are signs that the lack of beauty or elevation characteristic of modern regimes troubles reflective Americans of both the left and the right. For example, George Will, the prominent conservative pundit, has written a book the very title of which, *Statecraft as Soulcraft*, suggests a desire to transcend, or at least supplement, the modern politics of material well-being. Will writes that "liberal democratic societies are ill founded" because of their refusal to bridle "egoistic motives" and their concomitant neglect of the spiritual or moral needs of man.[60] The same dissatisfaction is suggested by the title of liberal commentator Michael Lerner's *The Politics of Meaning*, which argues for a public life that gets beyond "the dominant ethos of selfishness and materialism" and thus satisfies the "hunger for meaning and purpose in life."[61] As Plato, Aristotle, Rousseau, and Nietzsche teach us, however, such longings can only be realized through the political use of music to beautify the souls of individuals and thereby ennoble the life of the community.

Moreover, one may doubt whether the modern teaching of such as Hobbes, Locke, and Montesquieu is actually capable, at least in the long run, of securing even the more modest ends of safety and comfort to which they limit politics. As we have seen, these philosophers dispense with musical education in moderation, believing that they have discovered more reliable means of shaping human behavior in ways compatible with public order. Rather than use character formation to teach each citizen to control his passions, they instead emancipate passion and seek to use its energy to control its own destructiveness, devising elaborate institutional structures that secure the public good by using self-interest to check self-interest.

One cannot help but admit and even admire the ingenuity of such a project. Going further, one cannot help feeling some sympathy for the early moderns' judgment that the musical political teaching of Plato and Aristotle is problematic and that some alternative is required. Machiavelli may be wrong to suggest that what cannot be seen cannot be true, that because the "republics" of the ancient philosophers never existed in practice they must be merely imagined.[62] The truth of those propositions depends upon an argument that he does not make, and much that is respectable in the history of man's attempts to make sense of the world affirms the truth of things unseen and even unseeable. But Machiavelli is certainly right in his factual claim that the republics of the ancients have never been seen in practice. And it is not altogether unreasonable for him and his followers to suspect that something that has never existed in practice cannot be a very useful as a guide to practice.

In spite of all these concessions, however, one still wonders whether the political project of the early moderns will actually work. Will the emancipation and institutional management of selfish desire succeed in securing the public peace necessary for the satisfaction of man's desires for, in Hobbes's words, his "preservation" and "delectation"? Can we dispense with character formation and still achieve a stable social order? Here again we must qualify the question by asking whether such a project will succeed "in the long run." For, as was suggested earlier, it would be difficult to deny the considerable success the liberal societies of Europe and America have so far had in generating domestic peace and prosperity.

Such doubts about the ultimate feasibility of the modern project have been nourished on the suspicion that liberal modernity's initial success cannot be entirely attributed to modern political teaching. Some analysts, usually of a traditionally conservative frame of mind, have contended that liberal political regimes have been able to dispense with character formation without any apparent harmful effect only because of the vitality of certain private beliefs and institutions, like religion, that continue to teach moderation. But, such critics fear, we will soon begin to see the consequences of the public abandonment of character and moderation. In the face of the most authoritative institution's indifference to such concerns—which must ultimately appear as the indifference of the community itself, which the government represents—private institutions will be unable to sustain their commitment to teaching virtue. Then the social order that was maintained not by but despite modern arrangements will begin to decay.

Such criticisms of liberal modernity are rooted in an understanding of politics that has illustrious origins. For, as we have seen, Plato and Aristotle insist that character formation is necessary not only to the lofty ultimate ends of politics in the best political order, nobility of soul and refinement of mind, but also to the more modest aims of average cities, the maintenance of peace and the stability of the regime. Moreover, the ancient position is supported by a growing conviction, not just among traditional conservatives, that in America, the preeminent modern liberal society, the social fabric is becoming frayed and cannot be repaired by reliance on "political architecture" alone, that in addition to passion-manipulating institutions we need some degree of passion-moderating character formation, if the ends of the regime are to be attained. We have begun to see respected political scientists of both conservative and liberal inclinations addressing the connection between character and the stability of liberal democratic politics: James Q. Wilson in *On Character* and William Galston in *Liberal Purposes*.

In the light of this growing sense of the insufficiency of the politics of self-interest, one is forced to wonder whether the early moderns erred not only in their neglect of character formation generally but also more particularly in their neglect of music. If music's influence over the soul, over passion and action, is as potent as the musical political philosophers teach—and there is ample evidence that it is—then the founders of modern liberalism have neglected a powerful force that has the capacity to make or mar their political project. On the one hand, in its capacity to calm the passions music could serve as a useful supplement to the "political architecture" by which the moderns seek to control the effects of self-interested desire. On the other, in its ability to whip men into a passionate frenzy music could contribute to wildly irrational behavior that modern political institutions might prove unable sufficiently to contain.

With regard to the latter possibility, it may be that the early moderns—ironically, in light of their claim to offer a hardheaded political realism superior to the supposed utopianism of the ancient elevation of reason—actually *overestimate* human rationality. The moderns think that material inducements and deterrents manipulated by institutions will be equal to the task of maintaining order because they assume that reason will reliably lead men to do what is in their material self-interest. In so assuming, they may have underestimated the power of the spirited part of the soul, which can lead men to do things that are, from the standpoint of a concern with material well-being, irrational. As Socrates says in the *Republic*, men will endure all kinds and degrees of physical pain—"hunger, cold and everything of the sort"—when their spirit is sufficiently provoked.[63] Indeed, it is precisely because of its capacity for a noble indifference to the good of the body that Rousseau and Nietzsche embrace spiritedness as the cure for what they regard as the vulgar hedonism of the politics of liberal modernity.

As we have seen, moreover, Rousseau's and Nietzsche's turn to spiritedness, is intimately related to their return to music. They realized, like the ancients, that while certain kinds of music can calm spiritedness others can inflame it—and they ardently embraced the latter. The problem for the liberal societies founded on the principles of early modern political philosophy, then, is that in their neglect of music they could be unpleasantly surprised by a kind of music that, by stimulating spiritedness to a fever pitch, leads to behavior that is very destructive and that such societies, in their reliance on material incentives, cannot deter.

That there are still people susceptible to excessive spiritedness is suggested by numerous recent spectacular crimes, such as the infamous 1999 shooting spree at Columbine High. Such acts, originating in anger and resentment, obviously arise not from bodily desire but instead from the spirited passions excited to a frenzied level of self-assertion. Hence, they could not have been deterred by the appeal to material self-interest. The spirited character of such acts, and their resistance to the usual liberal solutions, is made even more plain by the way such crimes typically end: with the suicide of the murderer. Physically healthy people who deliberately plan the destruction of their own bodies are clearly not to be deterred by appeals to material self-interest.

The early moderns might respond that political philosophy needs to take its bearings from what is typical rather than atypical and therefore, that their amusical politics is good enough: people in whom spiritedness dominates so completely that they are deaf to the desires of the body are very rare. No doubt such people are rare. But they seem to be growing less rare. At least, one suspects that "senseless" violence—that is, violence in which modernity sees no sense because it arises from no desires that modernity can comprehend—attracts so much comment because it happens more often than it used to. In any case, the scarcity of such people is cold comfort, because they do not have to exist in very large numbers seriously to disturb our comfort and security.

Whose Music?

In the face of these problems associated with the politics of early modern political philosophy we turn to Plato and Aristotle, Rousseau and Nietzsche. Yet even here we find no easy answers, for we are still confronted with the great gulf between the ancient and late modern teachings. If music is necessary for the health of society, what kind of music? Indeed, what makes for the true health of the soul and the polity: the quieting of the passions and the flourishing of reason or

the silencing of reason and its replacement with passionate commitment? Once again, then, we are faced with the need to judge between
two radically different accounts of man, music, and politics.

One cannot help noticing the dangers of turning, with Rousseau
and Nietzsche, to a musical politics of nobility divorced from the
moderating influence of reason. In the thought of the ancients the
longing for excellence or nobility is kept decent—kept, that is, from
degenerating into merely the desire to assert one's own or one's
community's superiority—by the recognition, made possible by
graceful rhythm and harmony's cultivation of reason, of moral limits established by nature. Hence, for example, Aristotle argues in the
Politics that, although a wider sphere of rule does provide a greater
opportunity for the virtuous action which gives rise to happiness,
happiness cannot be gained through conquering those who by nature
deserve to be ruled as equals. For actions that are contrary to nature
are neither noble nor productive of happiness.[64] And Socrates' attempts to foster in the guardians not only the spirited love of victory
through gymnastics but also through music to make it submit to the
guidance of reason and thus render it compatible with the demands
of justice among citizens, as well as the natural well-being, the health
of soul, of the guardians themselves.

But the music of Rousseau and Nietzsche, as we have seen, seeks
to foster nobility by exciting rather than calming the passions, by silencing rather than awakening the reason. Specifically, it looks to
erect this new nobility on the foundation of what Plato terms the
spirited element of the soul. One wonders whether a nobility so
founded can be kept from turning into a kind of admirable barbarism—admirable because of its transcendence of the petty desires for
security and comfort which animate modern politics, but barbaric
because separated from the restraining reason of the ancients.

Rousseau scholar Christopher Kelly points out that a danger inherent in the passionate musical speech advocated by Rousseau is that
it "can be used to inspire unwholesome fanaticism instead of salutary

citizenship."[65] Yet one wonders if there is any important difference between fanaticism and the citizenship Rousseau thinks salutary. Music inculcates selfless citizenship giving rise to a kind of happiness that is a political approximation of the blissful experience of musically communicated moral love in savage society. Rousseau warns, however, that because moral love is necessarily accompanied by a fierce jealousy, this "tender and gentle sentiment" will receive "sacrifices of human blood."[66] The savage lover will kill mercilessly for the sake of his beloved. But the same will be true of the passionately patriotic citizen. We are thus reminded that the cities to which Rousseau points as models of political excellence, Rome and Sparta, were known not only for dedicated citizenship but also for ruthless imperial ambition.

The same danger is present in Nietzsche's thought. *The Birth of Tragedy* suggests that Dionysian music is useful because of its ability to foster nobility, understood as a passionate commitment to a culture, a way of life or ethical teaching presented in a dramatized myth. Yet Nietzsche is silent about the content of the ethical teachings of such myths, and that silence seems necessary in light of his assertion of the unintelligibility of the cosmos, which implicitly denies the possibility of any rational standard by which to judge the propriety of our passionate commitments. Thus, passionate commitment itself is more the basis of nobility than the intrinsic goodness of that to which one is committed. True, Nietzsche hopes that tragedy will produce—presumably by teaching simultaneously the nobility and the ultimate futility of passionate striving—a kind of political moderation, that tragic culture will strike a mean between two undesirable extremes: the inert otherworldliness of India and the this-worldly ambitiousness of Rome. Yet it is not clear that Nietzsche's teaching provides solid grounds for sustaining such moderation. After all, if one affirms musical tragedy's presentation of nature as passionate striving unguided and unchecked by reason, it seems likely that one will be inclined to choose, as most in harmony with nature, a life of passionate striving unguided and unchecked by reason. Again, on this view it is the intensity of the passion, and not the justice of the goal, that makes for human excellence. Perhaps it is this tendency in his thought that led Nietzsche later in life to suggest that Caesar and Napoleon are examples of the "highest human beings."[67]

It would seem, then, that these critics of early modernity, however justified their distaste for the lowness of modern politics, provide no safe alternative to it. We are thus compelled to turn to the ancients. And in the musical political philosophy of Plato and Aristotle we happily find a teaching that, by giving each element of human nature its due, offers the goods associated with the early and late modern accounts while avoiding their dangers.

Obviously there is a certain virtue to the political philosophy associated with Hobbes, Locke, and Montesquieu. These thinkers seek to ground politics on the desires of the body, and the satisfaction of those desires is in fact an important part of our happiness. After all, who wants a politics that neglects the good of the body? Plato and Aristotle, however, despite their lofty concerns with nobility of character and refinement of mind, do not offer such a politics. In fact, bodily well-being plays an important role in their teaching insofar is it is a necessary condition of the loftier goals they pursue. As Socrates notes in the *Republic*, a sick body is no less an impediment to the highest life than the excessive excitation of the bodily desires, and an important way to avoid both problems is to give the body what it needs.

Nonetheless, the partisans of the flesh might respond, the ancients, while they do not exactly deny the body's desires, do impose restraints on them that go beyond what most people will gladly endure. After all, the body likes to have not just what it needs but more; and this the ancients will not allow. This is undeniable, but it is essential to recognize that Plato's and Aristotle's musical education in moderation does not aim merely to establish restraint of the passions for its own sake but is instead directed toward the well-being of the whole man. For the indulgence of the bodily desires beyond what is necessary does not lead to any lasting satisfaction but only to a passing pleasure followed by a desire for more. Put simply, the desires of the body are insatiable and therefore cannot be the basis of a settled happiness. Moreover, the calming of the passions is necessary to the flourishing of reason, to our capacity to enjoy other, more human pleasures, less immediate but no less deeply rooted than those associated with the body. Thus classical political philosophy, unlike the philosophy of liberal modernity, cares for, without putting itself in the service of, the desires of the body, acknowledging what man has in common with animals without reducing him to the level of an animal.

The virtues of Rousseau and Nietzsche appear most clearly in contrast to the vices of their early modern predecessors. In its call for a politics that once again transcends the desires of the body and inspires men to a loyalty to something beyond themselves, their teaching seems an oasis of nobility gratefully encountered after passing through a desert of vulgarity. Yet, the ancient teaching of Plato and Aristotle is no less able to achieve these goods, and its does so without encountering the perils of the late modern approach. A noble transcendence of the desires of the body can be achieved by the musically fostered rule of reason in the soul as well as by the dominance of spiritedness, and the former approach avoids the latter's tendency to turn into an admirable but barbaric fierceness. At the same time, however, the classical account provides ample room for the activity and satisfaction of the spirited part of the soul. As the *Republic* teaches, reason rules in the soul only with the assistance of spiritedness, and in achieving moral nobility and wisdom, the goals of reason, a man gratifies the spirited desire for honor as well. Just as a dog is both restrained and ennobled by having a good man for a master, so the dog-like quality of spiritedness within us is restrained and ennobled by being placed, by the ancients' rearing in music, in the service of something higher than itself: the rule of reason in the soul and in our actions.

Finally, the classical teaching offers these advantages in a spirit of political moderation and flexibility. For although Plato and Aristotle have a clear conception of what is politically best, they are by no means doctrinaire in insisting that the best be achieved by everyone in all situations. They are as well aware as their critics of the rarity of, and hence the undeniable difficulty of achieving, in both individuals and cities, the qualities their political teaching seeks to foster. Their teaching is offered not as an ultimatum but as a standard by which to orient our political strivings, coming as close to it as circumstances permit. Thus the ancients combine their lofty aspirations with modest expectations without abandoning either.

Having judged the ancients to be the most reliable guides among the philosophers whose teachings we have explored, we may now turn once again to the contemporary controversies recounted in the introduction and see what clarity we can bring to them by analyzing them in light of Plato's and Aristotle's understanding of man, music, and politics.

∞ 8 ∞

Hungry Souls

THE CURRENT CONTROVERSY over pop music mirrors the ancient concern with music's ability to make or mar our capacity for both moral and intellectual virtue. For the debate concerns both the impact of popular music on the character and behavior of the young, as well as on their capacity to acquire a liberal education.

Before exploring these issues we may note that the classical teaching sounds a salutary note of caution applicable to participants on both sides. For both Aristotle and Plato remind us that a sufficient discussion of music's impact on the soul presupposes a philosophical investigation. The former, in the *Politics*, says that in these matters we need to turn for guidance to "those in philosophy who have experience in the education connected with music."[1] Similarly, in the *Republic* Socrates points out that his account of the legislation governing music depends upon an investigation of the nature of virtue and vice themselves.[2] Put another way, before we can judge music's impact on the health of the soul, we need some idea of what truly constitutes health of soul.

Thus, the ancient account reminds all participants in the current controversy that the judgments they make about music—about its moral and intellectual harmfulness, helpfulness, or neutrality—presuppose an investigation of fundamental questions. Such an inquiry is necessary if we are to avoid mindlessly and indignantly blaming what we do not like and praising what we do, as opposed to discovering what is truly conducive to, and what truly destructive of, human well-being. Thus we realize the need to seek guidance from political philosophy. But this realization necessarily induces caution or moderation. For in turning for instruction to political philosophers, whose theoretical concern with the truth about man and politics goes far beyond our own more immediate interests, both sides face the danger that their teachers may side with their enemies, or at least that those teachers will end up vindicating neither side without qualification.

Vulgarity as Vice

What light does the ancient account shed on the question of rock music's relationship to liberal education understood as the study of the traditional humanities? This question, as we have seen, is addressed very differently by Allan Bloom, who views rock as hostile to the traditional humanities and therefore bad, and Robert Pattison, who thinks rock incompatible with the traditional humanities but still defensible insofar as it can be the basis of a new and more authentically democratic kind of humanities.

Turning first to Pattison, we find a striking opposition to the musical teaching of the ancients. To a certain extent Pattison agrees with Bloom's characterization of rock. As the musical expression of vulgarity, rock is for Pattison at least the music of feeling generally, if not, as Bloom contends, the music of sex specifically—although even Pattison's treatment suggests, and he certainly makes no effort to deny, that sexual desire and the joys of its satisfaction loom large among rock's favorite topics. In any case rock is the music of passionate feeling, and it holds that man is fundamentally a passionate being. Thus it denigrates the refinements of mind, the treatment of the activity of reason as and end in itself, as inimical to human well-being. Pattison's recognizes rock's hostility to the traditional humanities.

In the end, however, Pattison, unlike Bloom, embraces the "triumph of vulgarity" of his book's title. His work concludes with a derisive dismissal of conservative calls to protect or revive the old liberal learning, with its emphasis on refinement and its upward gaze toward the transcendent, and instead calls for a new humanities based on the vulgarity of rock. Needless to say, this is not a position that the ancients could endorse.

Indeed, the very attempt to found the humanities on the vulgar spirit of rock music looks questionable in light of the ancients' identification of intellect or reason as the element in us that is distinctively human. On Pattison's account, rock treats man as at his core a passionate being and thus banishes reason to the periphery of human nature. Herein lies the problem: How do you have a humane learning—that is, a study that is somehow proper to human beings as human beings—that effectively dispenses with that which makes man man? Put another way, how do you have humanities based on what men have in common with animals: passion? In fact, if man is fundamentally passionate and therefore not essentially different from the beasts, being only more clever, it is not clear why we should not simply dispense with the humanities altogether rather than trying to reinvent them on the basis of rock's vulgarity. Why not just sit back and enjoy the mindless satisfactions of unrestrained feeling, rather than seeking to reflect on them?

One might respond that Pattison's rock-based vulgar humanities are, despite their elevation of passion, still capable of giving an account of and expression to distinctively human longings. The feelings that rock celebrates, one might contend, are not merely gross bodily desires but the "passions of the heart" discussed by Rousseau and held by him to be the core of human nature. After all, Pattison traces the roots of vulgarity to romanticism, of which Rousseau is thought to be one of the most famous proponents.

It is not clear, however, that such a response would actually solve the problem. The passions of the heart, as we argued earlier, bear a striking resemblance to the spirited desires discussed in the *Republic*. Yet, as Socrates points out there, such desires, unlike the longings of reason, are not unique to humans: horses and dogs, for example, are thought to be spirited. And we know from common experience that many animals do display such spirited qualities as anger, affection, loyalty, pride, and even a desire to dominate their fellows. At any rate, however one defines the feelings to which rock gives expression, the difficulty remains even on Pattison's own account. Rock, he admits, embraces "animalism" as a virtue.[3]

We might also question whether Pattison's new humanities would actually possess the virtues that he attributes to vulgarity. The thrust of his defense of vulgarity is that although it is by no means elevated or grand, it nonetheless displays certain solid, decent virtues the attractiveness of which cannot be denied. Indeed, his argument seems to be that vulgarity's virtues mirror its vices, that its very lowness is salutary, provided one looks at it in the right way.

From the apparent vice of vulgarity's abysmal lack of discrimination, Pattison gleans the virtue of its supposedly infinite tolerance. The vulgarian, he writes, "finds room in his universe for the atheist and the witchdoctor as well as the Pope and the rabbi."[4] But it was only a few years after the appearance of Pattison's book that rocker Sinead O'Connor created a brief sensation by concluding a performance on *Saturday Night Live* by tearing up a picture of John Paul II. This episode, moreover, cannot be dismissed as the exceptional act of an erratic personality and hence not truly indicative of the spirit of rock music. Rock, as Pattison points out, is the music of unbridled feeling. As such rock is fiercely intolerant of at least one thing: any assertion of the reality of the transcendent and its relevance to human life. Rockers sense, and rightly, that such notions would give authority to reason to place restraints on passion, and they therefore resist any person who dares to assert any variation on this teaching, whether Plato or the Pope.

There is even evidence of this intolerance in Pattison's own account of rock. At one point he presents a lyric from a song by the Police, hardly one of the more intemperate rock acts, as illustrative of rock's general belief that articulate speech is necessarily despotic: "the tyrants of language use words to create refined, transcendent laws which they impose on the wholesome chaos of the mind."[5] This, then, is the limit to vulgarity's tolerance: it is open to everything except the fundamental alternative to its own ideology.

Pattison's apology for vulgarity proceeds, transforming other of its seeming vices into virtues. While the refined might condemn it as "viciously cheap," one can at the same time say that it "appreciates life" as it is. Again, though rock's vulgarity might to some appear "selfish and sensuous," it can also be praised as "pragmatic and pleasant."[6] The ancient musical and political teaching, however, calls into question the pleasantness of vulgarity. The argument of the *Republic*, for example, would indicate that rock's vulgarity, by confining man to the realm of passionate feeling, condemns him to experience only the imperfect, transient shadow pleasures of the desiring part of the soul, while cutting him off from the more lasting and fulfilling satisfactions of the activity of reason.

Of course, one might well respond that to be persuaded of the superior pleasure of the life advocated by Plato and Aristotle one must accept their account of the soul and its relationship to the cosmos, an account that rock rejects, holding instead that human beings are fundamentally passionate beings living "in a universe of sensual experience."[7] Yet even the philosopher whose thought manifests a certain kinship with rock's ideology perceives that such an account of man and nature provides at best only an equivocal basis for pleasure. Pattison says that the vulgarity of rock is "full of infinite longings."[8] As Nietzsche's thought suggests, however, for a being of infinite longing in a universe of infinite longing, there can be no pleasure unmixed with pain. The absence of transcendent reason, of an intelligible order to nature, both frees passion from any limits and at the same time takes away the possibility of any final satisfaction, and thus the experience of life in such a universe is at once one of joy and anguish.

Finally, in what the refined might take as the defect of vulgarity's frivolity, Pattison finds the saving advantage of "a sense of humor."[9] Vulgarity, he says, is "funny."[10] No doubt this should, in all seriousness, be counted as a considerable virtue. Life would be rather dreary without humor, and it does have something distinctively human about it: only human beings make jokes. Nevertheless, Pattison overrates its importance in this context. The point of its sense of humor contributes to a defense of vulgarity only insofar as vulgarity alone possesses this virtue, but this is manifestly not the case. One need be only passingly familiar with the history of Western thought to know of many great figures famous for their belief in the transcendent and in the importance of refinement who nonetheless were very funny. Thomas More, celebrated for both his piety and his wit, springs instantly to mind.

Going further, we might note that such humorous effect as vulgarity achieves is only possible in the presence of some at least tacit acknowledgement of the importance of refinement. Both the blues and rock alike, Pattison notes, produce humor from the same material: the unruly desires of our lower nature. But while the former views these things with ironic detachment, the latter treats them with "urgency and overstatement."[11] Thus rock "makes its comedy out of the overindulgence of vulgarity."[12] To this extent the blues is more refined than rock, but even rock's humor owes a debt to the transcendent. For the overindulgence on which rock bases its comedy, the excessive commitment to our lower desires, only looks funny to the extent that it appears to us as ridiculous, as unworthy of a human being. That is, the absurdity of such things only comes to light insofar as we at least implicitly admit that we are more than passionate feeling and hence that we ought not treat such pleasures as if they were the beginning and end of human well-being.

If, in contrast, we were fully to hand ourselves over to vulgarity, then the overindulgence of such things could no longer appear funny, for then we would take them far too seriously. Take for instance our appreciation of Homer Simpson, that brilliantly depicted and unfailingly hilarious fictional exemplar of American vulgarity. Homer's adventures appear funny only because we are able to look down on him, and we can look down on him only because we can recognize, in the light of our implicit acknowledgement of the real importance of the transcendent, the absurdity of his intense devotion to the trivial pleasures of the body. If we were vulgar like Homer, then we would see things as he sees them: but he does not find his own life funny. If we shared his concerns then his anguish at finding the doughnut box empty would not amuse but would instead take on the aspect of tragedy.

In the end, then, the vulgar spirit of rock, on which Pattison hopes to base a new and more democratic humanities, is both dehumanizing and incapable of sustaining even the low virtues for which he praises it. Moreover, he is led into these difficulties by his failure to appreciate the natural power of music and its relationship to politics as presented by the ancients. Pattison makes what he can out of vulgarity because he thinks its triumph inevitable, insofar as it arises from the democratic nature of our civilization. He fails to consider, in the first place, the necessity of resisting vulgarity regardless of its significant advantages, since, as Aristotle reminds us, the complete victory of the spirit of democracy, unchecked desire, will mean democracy's self-destruction. Moreover, he neglects the possibility that such resistance is possible and fruitful because of a refined music's natural capacity to stimulate the soul's natural longing for the transcendent. Whatever the soul-deforming power of an imperfect regime's principles, nature is the always present ally whose aid we can enlist in preserving and improving such regimes.

Sweet Music and Sweet Reason

Turning to Allan Bloom, one is struck by the considerable sympathy with which Plato and Aristotle would no doubt view his condemnation of rock. Bloom's criticism is based on the notion that music should be used to prepare the soul for the activity of reason by attaching the immature passions to conceptions of the beautiful and sublime and thus drawing the soul in its maturity to the liberal study of such elevated things. Rock, however, appeals only to raw sexual desire and therefore teaches the young that sexual satisfaction is all, thus threatening to cut them off forever from the pleasures of intellect.

The ancients, as we have seen, also believe that music should be employed to prepare the soul for philosophic activity, and clearly they would reject rock's preoccupation with sexual pleasure not only as incompatible with that goal but also as hostile to moral nobility. On their view, an education in such music would produce not human flourishing but rather slavery to the desiring part of the soul. Such similarities between Bloom and the ancients are not surprising. For Bloom, in addition to generally taking Plato as his teacher in all educational matters, explicitly acknowledges the influence of Plato's teaching on music in the section of *The Closing of the American Mind* dealing with rock.

Closer inspection, however, reveals that Bloom's account departs considerably from that of the ancients. In addition to his criticism of rock on the basis of his belief that the right kind of music can prepare the soul for the activity of reason, Bloom also incongruously presents music itself—all music and not just rock—as the enemy of reason. "Music," he writes, "is the soul's primitive and primary speech" and is not only "not reasonable" but also actively "hostile to reason."[13] Even in its most refined and seemingly reasonable forms, he continues, the balance of music "is always tipped, if ever so slightly, toward the passionate."[14] Apparently, however, this inclination toward passion, no matter how slight, is always more than sufficient to render music implacably opposed to the demands of reason. Thus Bloom continues that, "armed with music, man can damn rational doubt. Out of the music emerge gods that suit it, and they educate men by their example and their commandments."[15]

Even more striking is Bloom's attribution of his understanding of music to both Plato and Nietzsche. Bloom asserts that "Plato's teaching about music," with which Nietzsche in *The Birth of Tragedy* "in large measure agrees," is, "put simply, that rhythm and melody, accompanied by dance, are the barbarous expression of the soul." Similarly, he elsewhere contends that for Plato "music expresses the dark, chaotic forces of the soul."[16] For both Plato and Nietzsche, we are to believe, "music is the medium of the *human* soul in its most ecstatic condition of wonder and terror."[17]

It is difficult to imagine any passage in the *Republic*—or any other dialogue—upon which Bloom could plausibly base such assertions about the Platonic understanding of music. To be sure, the *Republic* suggests that some kinds of music fit the description Bloom offers. But then it also indicates, as we have seen, that there is a graceful and orderly music that speaks to reason itself, awakening and stimulating its natural desire for intelligible order and preparing it for the mature and complete enjoyment of such order found in philosophic contemplation. It is difficult to see how such an art can be judged to be so completely and necessarily a manifestation of the "dark and chaotic" forces of the soul.

Less egregious is Bloom's association of such notions with Nietzsche, but even here he leads us astray. Of course, Nietzsche's Dionysian music, the expression of man and nature's passionate striving and its attendant joy and agony, does resemble Bloom's music of the soul's primitive condition of ecstatic terror and wonder. Nietzsche endorses such music and even goes so far to suggest that in some sense it alone is *real* music. Yet he nonetheless admits the existence and power of other kinds of music that calm the passions and foster a contemplative frame of mind. Such is Apollinian music.

These matters, moreover, represent more than academic quibbles over the proper interpretation of the texts in question. Consider, to begin with, the rhetorical difficulties attending Bloom's account. His discussion of rock says that all music is hostile to reason. Yet the book as whole teaches that the life of reason, of philosophic investigation, is the best life for man. Taken together, these two propositions powerfully convey the impression that Bloom thinks that music generally is a bad thing. Surely that which is hostile to that which is best is itself bad.

Of course, Bloom's discussion of rock also provides evidence that he is not unfriendly toward music. This is not, however, the understanding that many readers, and even many thoughtful ones, seem to have taken away from *The Closing of the American Mind*. Rather, it appears that the impression Bloom creates of his hostility to music is too powerful to be overcome by his assurances that some music can prepare the soul for the best life. Thus, among the critics of Bloom's book we find one writer of some erudition—enough to see the questionableness of Bloom's equation of the Platonic and Nietzschean musical teachings, and to offer a sophisticated account of the ways music can be said to appeal to reason—contending that rock is "only the occasion for Bloom to attack all music."[18] Similarly, in his commentary on Bloom, the late rocker Frank Zappa, a serious musician and one of the more articulate defenders of rock, argues that Bloom's account of music as the enemy of reason "is a puff pastry version of the belief that music is the work of the Devil: that the nasty ol' Devil plays his fiddle and people dance around and we don't want to see them twitching like that."[19]

This impression Bloom gives of having an animus against music creates formidable difficulties for his argument. After all, that music and the pleasure it gives are deeply rooted in our nature is a truth recognized not only by Bloom but also, as we have seen, by many political philosophers and much contemporary science. In addition, music is especially important to the young. In seeming to criticize music itself, Bloom invites readers to see him as a cranky old scold, implacably and ridiculously opposed to the aspirations of normal human beings generally and young people in particular. It should be no surprise that Bloom's argument gave rise to criticisms that it was at times "hyperbolic, meansprited, and fuddy-duddyish,"[20] as well as to dark suspicions that his book represents "a nasty, reactionary attack on the values of young people,"[21] an assault on "youth and its culture" revealing "a spirit that can hardly be called generous and a mind that can hardly be called open."[22]

In sum, Bloom's argument almost demands the average reader's hostility insofar as it seems to threaten to take rock away while offering nothing musical to take its place. And it is hard for people to be persuaded by an author who appears as a kind of mad surgeon who wants to amputate their favorite limb. That Bloom's statement of his case provokes such resistance is unfortunate, for his broader points— rock's hostility to human well-being and the possibility of and need for a music conducive to our flourishing—are, in light of the ancient account of music, worthy of serious attention.

Bloom's account, however, gives rise to theoretical as well as rhetorical difficulties, for it is far from clear that music as he understands it can reliably attain the ends he expects it to serve. If music appeals overwhelmingly to passion, as Bloom insists, how can it contribute to the soul's preparation for the life of reason? The answer to this question would appear to lie in Bloom's emphasis, elsewhere in *The Closing of the American Mind*, on the importance of opinion or prejudice as a necessary condition of one's attraction to liberal education. Those students Bloom calls "nice," who have drunk so deeply of moral relativism that they have no strongly held views, cannot feel the importance of the issues addressed by liberal education. Such learning presents itself as a search for the truth about the good; but such students already know that there is no "truth" about such things, only "values," a diversity of opinions all of equal validity. Hence their indifference to the traditional humanities. In contrast, according to Bloom, young people with prejudices, with firmly held opinions about the good, sense the importance of the issues explored by liberal education and therefore can be drawn to it. Thus it seems that for Bloom the value of music is that it can, by appealing to and sublimating the immature soul's "nascent sensuality," create a passionate attachment to certain ideas of the good that is the necessary condition of liberal education.[23]

Such a use of music seems more reminiscent of Rousseau and Nietzsche than Plato and Aristotle. This similarity, moreover, points to the difficulties involved in Bloom's account of how music can prepare the young for liberal education. For Rousseau and Nietzsche intend their music to generate convictions so passionately held as to be resistant to reason. That such music can serve the purposes Bloom has in mind is, to say the least, questionable. It could, as Bloom hopes, create in the young a sense of the importance of the issues explored by liberal education. On the other hand, it could just as easily accomplish too much, fostering a disposition that views such issues as too important to be subjected to liberal learning's rational scrutiny, or one blinded by the strength of its feelings to the possibility that such a process is even necessary. The products of Bloom's musical education are as likely as not to be mere ideologues, and thus as impervious to the charms of liberal education as their nicely indifferent, relativistic colleagues.

Ultimately, Bloom's concern with the capacity of the young for liberal education arises from his concern with their flourishing and their happiness, for he evidently regards the life of philosophic inquiry as the best and most satisfying. Here again, though, his account both departs from the ancient understanding and seems unable to achieve what he seeks. Plato and Aristotle, we recall, teach that an education in graceful and orderly music contributes to the soul's highest happiness by awakening and cultivating its natural love for the beautiful order of the cosmos, a love that is most completely satisfied in the activity of philosophic contemplation. Bloom, however, appears to shun such metaphysics and instead emphasizes the satisfaction that arises from reason's challenging and overcoming one's unreflectively held beliefs. Such an education is liberal in the sense that it liberates the student from his prejudices. The education Bloom offers, taken as a whole, presents the appearance of a very strange contraption: music creates in us a passionate attachment to certain opinions, and then liberal education gives us the satisfaction of being freed from those opinions.

It is not clear what positive pleasure is involved in such a process. Is there an order to the universe to which the soul is by nature attracted and in the enjoyment of which it finds its final satisfaction? Bloom does not clearly say, and his ambuguity creates doubts about whether his account establishes the happiness of the life of intellect on solid foundations. On the one hand, he does seem to speak of a natural satisfaction that arises from the grasping of "the intelligible order of nature as a whole."[24] Elsewhere, however, he appears to suggest that such intelligibility, and hence the pleasure that attends its contemplation, arises not so much from the nature of things as from culture. He says that in the absence of "the great revelations, epics and philosophies as part of our natural vision, there is nothing to see out there."[25] Indeed, Bloom flirts with nihilism, asserting "the lack of cosmic support for what we care about" and suggesting that the truth, far from being attractive, is rendered "tolerable" only by the pleasure of insight.[26] In the end Bloom's account of nature, no less than his account of music, seems more in line with Nietzsche's than Plato's. It thus points, contrary to his explicit intention, more emphatically to a repudiation, than to a vindication of, the life of reason.

Against Pop's Defenders

We turn at last to the more familiar branch of the current argument about popular music, that concerned with the influence of music on the moral character of the young and hence its consequences for the larger social and political order. Here one is struck most immediately by the evident agreement of the ancient political philosophers with the critics of such music. These critics fear that the immoderation of obscene and violent pop will make a lasting impression on the young, and the capacity of music to form character for good or ill is one of the cardinal points of the classical teaching. The critics fear that through its shaping of character such music's elevation of unrestrained passion will lead to an increase in social pathologies and perhaps finally to the collapse of, or at least to some drastic change in the character of, our civilization. Similarly, the ancients stress the contribution of musically induced moderation to the maintenance of public order and the possibility that its absence will result in the destruction of the regime.

This initial impression of the unqualified vindication of the critics is strengthened by the weakness of the position of the defenders of the popular music at issue. For, examined in light of the teaching of the *Republic* and the *Politics*, the arguments commonly deployed in defense of such music carry little weight.

In the first place, we recall, some have claimed that the concerns of pop's detractors are overblown because the musical obscenity to which they point is actually quite rare. We may pause to note, before considering the classical response, that this argument did not long remain in the arsenal of pop's public defenders, probably because of its demonstrable falsity. It seems to have been advanced once or twice in the context of the initial debate surrounding the efforts of the PMRC, only to have been quickly abandoned in the face of the considerable evidence to the contrary. Much of the explicit sexuality of which the PMRC complained in 1985 was found not in the music of underground rock acts whose names most of us would not recognize but instead in the hit albums of such widely popular bands as the Rolling Stones, Kiss, and Mötley Crüe.[27] Nor has the subsequent addition of violence to sex as a prominent theme pushed musical obscenity to the periphery of pop. Thus in the 1990s such rap and rock groups as N.W.A., Guns N' Roses, 2 Live Crew, DMX, and Master P have achieved great commercial success.[28] Whatever else pop music obscenity may be, it is clearly not marginal.

Even if such music were considerably less a mainstream phenomenon than it apparently is, however, it would still, according to Plato and Aristotle, be a source of serious corruption. In order to appreciate this we need to refer to the classical conception of the regime. This term is used somewhat equivocally in classical political thought, referring broadly to the whole way of life of a community as well as more narrowly to the arrangement of the ruling offices. For the ancients, however, the two definitions are related. As Aristotle points out, the actions and attitudes of the ruling element, those upon whom the arrangement of offices bestows political authority, set the intellectual and moral tone for the whole society, since all look up to its members as worthy to exercise rule. This phenomenon, moreover, is present even in modern egalitarian societies in which the majority rules. The citizens of a democracy, as Tocqueville observes, are predisposed to accept the opinions of the majority as true.

On this understanding, once the existence and marketing of obscene music becomes publicly known, the ruling element's reaction will set the tone for the whole society's attitude toward it. In a democracy, if such music goes unchallenged by the majority, it implies society's judgment that it is a matter of indifference. For the classical political philosophers, however, such a response, or rather non-response, would enlist the regime's tacit cooperation in the corruption of souls. By ignoring music's well-known moral miseducation of even a few citizens, it would teach all that such miseducation is not a very serious matter. But such a teaching is itself a kind of corruption. The critics of contemporary pop seem instinctively to understand this problem. Hence their desperate attempts, through public exposure and criticism, to provoke some kind of majority repudiation of such music, expressed in letter writing campaigns or economic boycotts.

Obscene popular music has also been defended on the grounds that, even if its content is morally questionable, the young are immune to any harm that might arise from it because they generally pay no attention to the lyrics. This argument, and indeed the entire debate's preoccupation with lyrics, misses a key point of the ancient teaching, which claims that people generally and the young especially are influenced most powerfully not by the words of a song but by the music itself, the rhythm and harmony and tune. These, says Socrates in the *Republic*, lay hold of the soul most powerfully and bring grace or its opposite with them. For Plato and Aristotle, the ethical effect of the music to which the bodies of young Americans gyrate—on the dance floor, in their cars, in their rooms, and as they walk down the street—would be no less disastrous if it were purely instrumental. The music itself, not the words, causes the gyrations of passion in the soul that show themselves in the movements of the body. Such experiences, repeated often during one's formative years, leave a lasting mark. And the immoderation such music fosters, Plato and Aristotle remind us, tends necessarily toward injustice, whether or not the words of the songs explicitly advocate it.

Indeed, such is the power of rhythm and harmony, on the ancient account, that such music would foster immoderation and injustice even if the lyrics advocated their opposites. Hence, we see not only the radical insufficiency of the critics' efforts to address the problem merely by expunging a few dirty words but also the questionableness of attempts to impose on such music a "positive message" of social responsibility or Christian virtue.[29] A pornographic film arouses excessive sexual desire, necessarily tending toward the vices of fornication and adultery, even if by its dialogue it purports to depict a married couple engaging in what is for them an act of virtue. Such

is the power of the visible image, and such is the power of intemperate music, no matter what the words may convey.

Some have tried to dismiss the fears of the critics of pornographic
pop by claiming that such music is quite harmless because music does
not change the way people behave. Occasionally this point is supported by an appeal to anecdotal evidence: an acquaintance is identified who, it is said, loves the most offensive forms of popular music
and immerses himself in it daily, yet is the most gentle and civilized
of men—or at least not a rapist and a murderer. Of course, such an
argument is unconvincing. Many people can point to acquaintances
who chain smoke and still live to an advanced age with few health
problems. Such people, however, are exceptional, and this argument
says no more about the general physical impact of smoking than the
previous one says about the general moral impact of music.

More thoughtful commentators, however, have sought to advance
a more sophisticated defense of this position. Among them we find
Michael Linton, a professor of music theory and composition, writing in the generally conservative *First Things*. In fairness to Linton
and to *First Things* it should be pointed out that his aim is not to give
aid and comfort to the defenders of obscene pop music. It is instead
to refute the currently popular, and to Linton incredible, claims of the
salutary emotional, intellectual, ethical, and physical effects of listening to the music of Mozart.[30] Yet Linton, going after much bigger
game, also uses the occasion to attack Plato in particular as well as
the general notion that a certain kind of music can be ethically beneficial. Thus he dismisses the *Republic*'s account of music as "perhaps
the stupidest notion a great mind has ever come up with."[31]

On careful examination, however, we find that Linton's argument
does not truly refute, because it does not truly address, the classical
teaching on music and character. Looking to history, Linton points
to the failed attempt of Charles ix of France, apparently acting under the influence of Plato's musical and political thought, to calm sec-
tarian passions by promoting music. Charles, it seems, established

an Academy of Poetry and Music in the hope that "proper music-making would restore order to his land, ending the bloodshed between Catholic and Protestant." "Problem is," notes Linton, "it didn't work. French Protestants and Catholics did not lay down their arms and embrace each other upon hearing the strain of fifes playing music in the Dorian mode."[32]

Here Linton accomplishes nothing more than to erect and then knock down a straw man, for by making such an argument he implicitly attributes to the ancients a belief in the power of music they clearly do not profess. Nothing in the writings of Plato or Aristotle suggests that Charles's venture could be successful. Their emphasis, as we have seen, is on the impact that music has on character, and thereby on behavior, through its influence over time on the souls of the young, who are impressionable. On this basis they posit music's ability to contribute significantly to a decent public order. Never do they suggest that it could be powerful enough to retrieve such order once lost by instantly transforming the character of millions who had never received a proper habituation in the first place.

Linton concludes his argument, and summarizes his misunderstanding of the ancient position, by contending that music cannot "overcome the will."[33] "Music," he writes,

> is not a drug that incapacitates the listener and produces a predictable result. A whole lifetime spent listening to Bach will not automatically make a woman love God. And—despite the warnings of two generations of moralists—a lifetime listening to the Rolling Stones will not make a man fornicate. Particular kinds of music may express things that appeal to the listener, and the listener may select a particular kind of music because he finds that it resonates with his own—premusical—emotional condition, but the music itself can never cause the listener to act. Action is always a function of the will, and while music may prod, and it may suggest, it cannot force.[34]

Advancing this argument against the ancient teaching on music is a bit like saying that it is silly to worry about the effects of habitual viewing of x-rated movies on adolescent boys, since visual images cannot overpower the will. Of course, the ancients do not suggest that music, any more than pornography, can overpower the will—merely that both music and visual images can move the passions, and the former more powerfully than the latter. They also observe, however, that this power, exerted repeatedly over time on souls that are immature and impressionable, can produce a certain disposition of the passions and thereby influence action by making it easier or more difficult for reason to see, and for the will to choose, what is right. To deny this is to suggest, implausibly, that in human beings, who are embodied creatures, intellect and will exist in some kind of pristine isolation, utterly uninfluenced by the movements of the passions.

Staking out a similar position, Robert Pattison claims that rock is a merely mythical realm from which rockers derive emotional satisfaction but which has "little direct influence on ordinary behavior." "Any connection between rock music and the behavior of large numbers of people," he contends, "is unproven and probably unprovable." Dismissing the arguments of those who have sought to use the evidence of studies in social science to "support the contention that rock is a social menace," he claims on the contrary that "there is no genuine scientific evidence to support the moral's rap brought against rock."[35]

Pattison's demand for scientific proof of rock's moral influence, however, is merely a rhetorical sleight of hand. After all, Pattison's interesting and insightful book offers many generalizations, derived from the content of rock music, about the way rockers typically think and feel. Most of these generalizations ring true to the informed reader, and Pattison seems content to rely on that effect alone for the plausibility of his argument. Why, then, should this particular generalization about rock's influence on behavior—which also enjoys a kind of prima facie plausibility—have to justify itself at the bar of science when all of Pattison's generalizations do not?

No doubt Pattison is right in saying that science cannot come to the aid of those who worry about the social impact of rock, but that is only because of the way he sets the terms of the debate. The context of his argument on this point, which is introduced by an account of a study on the effects of listening to rock on students' emotional state while taking a test, suggests that by "science" Pattison means the knowledge that comes from controlled experiments exploring human behavior. There are, however, as we have seen, studies that do testify to the impact of music generally and rock specifically on the way people act. But Pattison demands scientific evidence showing that rock affects the actions of "large numbers of people," which evidence is, and always will be, unavailable, since such experiments can only be conducted on relatively small numbers of people. This effort to establish the debate on terms artificially favorable to Pattison's side, however, does nothing to diminish the reasonableness of the strictly unscientific, though eminently plausible, conclusion that if rock can influence the way a few people act, it can do so for larger numbers as well. This is especially true when we consider, again, that the ancient account emphasizes music's ability to shape action only through forming character over a long period of time, a process that is obviously not easily verifiable by social science, yet is, for all that, readily verifiable by the commonsense reasoning of the ancients: music moves the passions, the young are impressionable, so music that plays a prominent role in the lives of the young can form character, understood as a certain disposition of the passions, and thereby influence action.

Furthermore, even if Pattison is correct and rock music is nothing more than a fantasy lived in the mind of the rock devotee, it would still be, according to the classical teaching, a serious "social menace." This point is brought to light by the ancients' general emphasis on human flourishing in addition to social order, and more specifically by their account of the highest happiness that results from the activity of the human mind in leisure. As Aristotle teaches, leisure, whether or not it is understood and used rightly, is taken by most people to be the end or purpose of life. Serious people use it for the most serious activities, the labor of the intellect for knowledge desirable for its own sake, while less serious ones use it merely for play.[36] But both alike experience leisure as the center or core of life, or, putting it more strongly, as life or living itself. For most of us work is not done for its own sake but is merely the means to living, to the goods we enjoy in the time we can be free from work. Leisure is in contrast the time when we actually live, when we are free to enjoy the things that we would choose for their own sake. In sum, their leisure is what most people cherish most and is where they expect to find their happiness.

For Plato and Aristotle, however, the crucial issue is whether the things people enjoy in their leisure are truly worthy of us as rational beings and whether they are conducive to the happiness proper to such beings. In this light rock's mythical elevation of passionate feeling and denigration of reason—even if, as Pattison insists, sheer fantasy confined to the mind of the rocker—is ruinous insofar as it incapacitates the young for the kind of leisure that could be truly fulfilling. Rock music prepares the soul for, and then itself becomes, a leisure activity that is coarse, vulgar, and subhuman, and thus hostile to the highest happiness that we can achieve. Therefore, rock is on the ancient account an evil to be resisted—whether or not it inflicts material harm on society by making people into murderers or rapists, drug addicts or unprepared teenage parents.

What of the various defenses of sexually explicit and explicitly violent pop organized around the notion of such music as a kind of art? One such line of argument implies that beneath the admittedly rough exterior of much apparently immoral pop music there is, accessible at least to the sensitive listener, a much less objectionable, perhaps even wholesome, teaching. This argument, like the others we have examined, fails to allay the concerns the ancients would have with such music. Once again, Plato and Aristotle's emphasis is primarily on music's lasting impact on character through its influence on the young. The young, however, are singularly ill-equipped to discern whatever subtle positive message there may be in such music. As Socrates warns in the *Republic*, a good city will not allow the young to be exposed to immoral tales, "whether they are made" with or without a "hidden sense," because a "young thing can't judge what is hidden sense and what is not" and "what he takes into his opinions at that age has a tendency to become hard to eradicate and unchangeable."[37]

Furthermore, here the argument once again fails to account for the natural power of rhythm and harmony to lay hold of the soul. Thus, even if young listeners could discern the hidden meaning in the lyrics of such music, that would not significantly lessen the harm done to their souls by the effect of the music itself on their passions. Perhaps a given song explicitly depicting the violent life of a gang member actually intends to criticize that life. That does not alter the fact that by setting such a depiction to music the artist makes the listener take part in it. That is, by enhancing such an imitation with music— the power of which, the ancients warn, can make the soul feel passions—the artist induces the listener to *feel with* the person whose life is being imitated, which is another way of saying that musical imitations create sympathy for the life imitated. And as Socrates warns in the *Republic*, from such imitation comes "a taste for the being," an inclination toward the life depicted. For such "imitations, if they are practiced continually from youth onwards, become established as habits and nature, in body and sounds and in thought."[38] The argument that such music might have a more constructive message than it at first appears to have is a singularly inadequate defense of music that is both offensive on its face and marketed primarily to children and adolescents.

Another art-based defense casts the music in question as a powerful portrayal of harsh reality. This argument, as we noted in chapter one, depends on the notion, never defended but simply assumed, that it is the business of art to imitate life as it is, even in its uglier manifestations. On the basis of our exploration of music in the history of political philosophy, however, we can see that this assumption is at least questionable, that it has to contend with the existence of a very different, though not less intellectually respectable, account of the purposes of art rooted in the thought of Plato and Aristotle. For these classical thinkers, art should be in the service of human flourishing, should try to foster the moral and intellectual excellence in which rational beings find their highest happiness. Hence, for the ancients art should not imitate, and thereby create sympathy for, every human behavior indiscriminately.

This does not mean, we hasten to add, that such art as could meet with the ancients' approval would have to be a sanitized denial of the ugly side of human existence. Here the distinction Socrates makes in the *Republic* between simple narration, on the one hand, and imitation, on the other, is crucial.[39] The ancients do not say that art should not *tell of* evil, only that it should not *imitate* it. The bad things, Socrates says, are to be narrated or reported: the good poet will relate their essentials without depicting them in detail. What is not allowed, for reasons discussed already, is that the bad should be imitated and the souls of the listeners be drawn into the imitation through the use of music.

This defense of obscene pop as a powerful artistic communication of certain harsh realities is related to an understanding of the artist as a kind of raiser of social and political consciousness. For the ugly facts communicated by such music are, on this account, politically relevant, are in fact manifestations of unjust social circumstances that need to be politically redressed. Such a use of music, however, appears reminiscent of Rousseau and Nietzsche and thus is subject to all the same difficulties as theirs. After all, nobody would claim that the music in question seeks to calm the passions and awaken the reason. After all, as its critics and its proponents agree, contemporary popular music is the music of feeling. Rather, it seeks, like the music of Rousseau and Nietzsche, passionately to lay hold of the soul of the listener and make him feel what the musician depicts. The purpose of this is to stir up a passionate response to the concerns of the artist, ultimately to create a passionate commitment to the ideals the artist professes. The more politically serious the music, the more true this is.

Such a project—to try to win our support while suppressing our reason—has all the moral dignity of propaganda. Hence it raises the same question we confronted in the context of our discussion of the problems attending the Rousseauean and Nietzschean use of music: If reason is to be abandoned as useless to guide our aspirations, even as corrosive of the maintenance of noble aspirations, what limits can be placed on the uses to which music will be put? If passion is all there is, then on what basis do we condemn those who enlist music's persuasive power in the support of their own sincerely felt but nonetheless destructive passions? Why not use music to preach racism as well as to preach against it? That this is more than merely an academic difficulty is indicated by the presence of, and the pop world's apparent willingness to tolerate, anti-white and anti-Semitic racism in some rap music and anti-black racism in some heavy metal.

This presentation of obscene pop music as an artistic political statement also provides an opportunity for its defenders to go on the rhetorical offensive by presenting the efforts of the critics against such music as a kind of class-based power play. If the music in question is rap, then its moralistic critics can be painted as representatives of an oppressive white power structure trying to silence the political expression of the black underclass. If, on the other hand, the music in question is some form of hard rock dominated by white performers, then such critics can be cast as the representatives of despotic adult authority callously suppressing the musical expression of the psychic suffering of American youth.

In the first place, we should note that such arguments depend to a considerable extent on the assumption that such music is a responsible form of political communication. In light of the counter-arguments advanced above, they lose some of their force immediately. More profoundly, such arguments assume that there is no common good shared by those interested in intensely passionate musical expression and the guardians of social order who are necessarily suspicious of such expression. To put the case in starker terms, such arguments imply that the social order defended by the critics of explicit pop is beneficial to them but harmful to those whose passionate music seems to challenge that order. No doubt there is some truth in this, for obviously those who enjoy positions of authority in a given society have more personally to gain from the maintenance of its stability than those who do not enjoy authority. Therefore, the restraint on the passions needed to perpetuate that social order is not as burdensome to the former as it is to the latter. This is not, however, the whole story, as the ancient teaching on the politics of music instructs us. That teaching insists that there is some common good between the defenders of the social order and those who seem to chafe under its restrictions, for the moderation of passion that is the necessary condition of the stability and decency of society is equally the necessary condition of the flourishing and happiness of the individual, realized in the activities of moral and intellectual excellence.

Finally, as we noted in chapter one, the defenders frequently counter the critics by invoking the specter of censorship. For the most part, one notes in passing, the critics have in fact been careful not to call for government control of the music they condemn. Even if they did advocate censorship, however, the ancients would, as we have seen, agree with them. On their account some kind of censorship would be necessary at least to prevent such music from being the formative influence in the lives of the young. For its excessive agitation of the passions of the young, Plato and Aristotle would hold, threatens to create immoderate citizens and is therefore incompatible with the minimal requirements of social and political order, not to mention the basic conditions of moral and intellectual excellence. At this point we are tempted to discard the classical teaching on music and politics as utterly irrelevant to our current concerns, for censorship is utterly alien to the spirit of American politics.

We need not, however, come to this conclusion. For the aforementioned flexibility of the ancient account saves it from irrelevance to our particular situation. As we noted earlier, the classical political teaching possesses simultaneously lofty standards and modest expectations. Its spirit is not to insist that every community adopt censorship—or any other political or educational expedient it recommends—but rather to prod every community to strive, as much as its own circumstances permit, to achieve the conditions of human well-being as it is articulated by that teaching.

No doubt the prevailing interpretation of the First Amendment casts grave suspicion on the constitutionality of government regulation of music. No doubt most ordinary Americans would oppose such action. But the ancients still have a practical course of action to recommend to us. As Aristotle says in the *Nicomachean Ethics*, when moral education "is neglected by the community, it would seem to be the duty of the individual to assist his own children and friends to attain virtue."[40]   Thus the ancients would, in light of the practical impossibility of censorship, approve the very kind of action adopted by the critics of obscene and violent popular music: efforts to diminish the role of such music in the lives of children through public persuasion while pointedly shunning the use of governmental coercion.

A Classical Critique of Conservatives

Again, this discussion powerfully suggests that the ancient thinkers side substantially with the critics who assert the morally and socially problematic character of the music at the center of this controversy. We cannot help but notice, however, that the classical account provides the basis for a much more penetrating criticism of this music than the contemporary critics seem to have envisioned. This observation must give us pause, for it suggests that the grounds of the classical teaching's criticism of obscene pop differ from those of the contemporary critics. And that in turn raises the possibility that Plato and Aristotle would find fault with the position of such critics as well as with that of pop's defenders.

In fact, when we compare the ancients' musical and political teaching with the concerns raised by the contemporary critics, two striking differences emerge. First, the critics attack only the lyrics of such music, but, unlike the ancients, say nothing about the ethical character of the music itself. Our critics find no fault with the immoderate character of the music of the songs they condemn. At least, they find no *objective* fault with it: it may not be to their taste, but they appear unaware of any publicly credible moral complaint to make about it. Yet, the subtext of the critics's concern with music is, like that of the ancients, a belief in the moral and political importance of moderation or self-control, our capacity to restrain our passions. And as all the musical political philosophers teach, as much other evidence indicates, and as these critics are no doubt aware, music in the narrow sense does possess a remarkable power to agitate the passions. Why, then, the critics's apparent indifference to the passionate nature of such music? It seems that they lack the ancient thinkers' suspicion of excessive passion as in itself a danger to human well-being. For such critics the musical inducement of passionate frenzy in the young, and hence the fostering of an excessively passionate character in them, is unobjectionable, so long as that frenzy is not related by the words of the song to any manifestly anti-social behavior.

Thus comes to light the second striking difference between the ancients and the contemporary detractors of pop music: the critics' concerns are primarily negative, while those of the ancients are largely positive. That is, while the latter seek to enlist music in the support of the loftiest virtues, the former seek only to prevent it from fostering the most dangerous vices. Plato and Aristotle, as we have seen, offer a beautiful, graceful music that aims to calm the passions and awaken the reason, thus paving the way for the highest happiness that comes from the soul's enjoyment of the nobility of ethical virtue and the beauty of theoretical truth. The critics, in contrast, offer opposition to an ugly music that they fear fosters the most vicious depravity.

Most revealing, however, is the notion of the human good implied by the critics' understanding of the bad activities to which the music they condemn seems to lead. Up to this point we have characterized that good as social stability or public order. But public order for the sake of what? Consider the evils celebrated by the music usually singled out for criticism as a public menace: murder and rape. Such activities are a threat to our bodily integrity, which is implicitly understood to be good. Of course, such behaviors *are* in fact bad and bodily integrity *is* in fact an important human good. The point here, however, is the limited character of the human good implied by the discourse of the contemporary critics of violent and pornographic pop: there is nothing in their arguments pointing to any additional, higher, or more complete understanding of the good for man. The combined effect of what they emphasize and what they fail to acknowledge is to suggest that bodily integrity—put another way, comfortable self-preservation—is *the* good for man. Hence the considerable distance of their position from that of the classical political philosophers.

In the end, then, these critics seem to have more in common with the early modern, amusical political philosophers—with Hobbes, Locke, and Montestquieu—than with the musical ancients. For both contemporary conservatives and amusical philosophers, immoderate passion as such is not a threat to human well-being, for human well-being is not understood in any very lofty way. They do not, as the ancients did, conceive human well-being as the consummation in action and thought of reason's attraction to the objects of moral and intellectual excellence, which consummation requires the calming of passion. Instead, excessive passion is only problematic insofar as it leads to overt criminality, that is, to behaviors that tend to threaten harm to the body. In other words, immoderation is bad only to the extent that, in going too far, it undermines our ability to satisfy our desires. But on this view satisfaction of desire is itself the good, and passion is the realm in which human happiness is realized. Hence, even in their seemingly classical concern with character formation, the contemporary critics of pop music have more fundamentally in common with the early moderns than with the ancients.

To clarify these matters further, let us consider the significance of the term *kalon* in ancient political philosophy. This Greek term can be translated into English with equal correctness as either the "noble" or the "beautiful." Thus, for the ancients, virtue, that is, nobility of character and action, is beautiful, and as such is desirable for its own sake, apart from any material advantages that may follow from it. Hence the kinship in their thought between beautiful music and beautiful souls, and the belief in the former's capacity to generate the latter.

The political thinkers of early modernity, however, utterly reject this understanding of virtue. Hobbes derides the ancients for failing to see what virtue is good *for*. Far from being desirable for its own sake, it is instead merely useful, useful with a view to securing the conditions of one's "preservation" and "delectation." Virtue is the code of behavior requisite to the maintenance of peace. Locke stakes out essentially the same intellectual territory, claiming that the ancients failed to get any suitors for virtue because they failed to provide her with a dowry. Show men the material benefits to be gained from virtue, he contends, and their willingness to practice it will increase considerably.

Of course, as Locke and Hobbes well knew, the content of a virtue practiced for the sake of comfortable self-preservation would differ considerably from one sought for its own nobility. The former would be markedly lower than the latter: self-interested, calculating, pedestrian, but for all that solid, reliable, decent, and its attractiveness readily intelligible to all men—rather than grand, beautiful, difficult to achieve, and requiring a musical education in moderation that few, initially at least, would find agreeable. But, on the early modern teaching, the facts must be faced: human beings are fundamentally desiring creatures and therefore the ancient musical education and the character it produces are contrary to our nature and ultimately not satisfying.

This, in a nutshell, is the modern understanding, both as it appears in the works of the intellectual architects of modern liberalism and as it is implied by the arguments advanced by the contemporary critics of popular music. For, as we have seen, there is little in the position of these critics to suggest that virtue is noble or beautiful and hence choiceworthy for its own sake. There is, in contrast much—their apparent embrace of passion as the realm of human fulfillment, their emphasis on social order as protective of bodily safety, their silence on any higher good—indicating a fundamental kinship with the modern view of virtue as merely useful with a view to comfortable self-preservation. Hence these critics' failure to call for a beautiful music in the service of man's highest aspirations. The goodness of such aspirations, their contribution to human happiness, and music's relationship to them are all unintelligible on their understanding of human nature.

In the end, then, the musical political philosophy of Plato and Aristotle implies a criticism of the detractors—and one no less severe than that it implies of the defenders—of our morally offensive and socially destructive popular music. Viewed from the standpoint of the ancients, the position of these critics shares the fundamental flaw of the philosophy of their early modern intellectual forefathers:

it fails to do justice to man as man. In its dismissal of reason as man's true self and its attendant rejection of the longings of reason as the core of human happiness, in its single-minded emphasis on the satisfactions of bodily security and comfort, it reduces man to the level of an animal, and a rather timid one at that. In their failure to counter the savagery of contemporary rock and rap with a musical education in the service of distinctively human aspirations, such critics appear not as civilized men condemning barbarians but as sheep condemning wolves. No doubt the sheeps' complaints are understandable, but they certainly do not stem from any more elevated source than the wolves' appetites.

Hungry Souls

The critics might respond by appealing to the rhetorical necessities imposed by the prevailing culture. Such criticisms, they might say, perhaps have some validity in the realm of mere theory. But we are practical people—politicians, public activists, and opinionmakers—engaged in the practical work of resisting a form of music that presents a practical difficulty: a real threat to public decency and order. If we hope to make any public headway against such music, we must speak against it in terms intelligible to the public. But most people think of the good as bodily security and comfort and think of the bad as anything that threatens them. Most people would certainly regard any public call for a musical formation of the young with a view to the activities of moral and intellectual virtue, understood as good in themselves, as utterly ridiculous, naively high-minded—and perhaps even snobbish—nonsense. We cannot succeed in the public fight against this music by getting ourselves laughed at. In our battle against such music we appeal to a fundamentally modern, and therefore implicitly hedonistic, notion of the good because ours is a fundamentally modern nation in which that notion overwhelmingly prevails.

Whatever the difficulties caused by the loftiness of the classical account and the evident challenge it poses to our opinions and way of life, the more modern approach adopted by the critics is as ineffectual as it is low. Indeed, its theoretical failure to do justice to man as more than bodily appetite gives rise to its practical impotence in the face of the barbaric music from which it seeks to protect us. For liberal modernity itself both indirectly causes and is utterly unable to resist the savage popular music from which the critics hope to defend, and as an alternative to which they offer, liberal modernity.

In its account of human nature, liberal modernity, of which the conservative critics of pop are only the most recent popular proponents, fails to do full justice to man. Life in societies organized on modern principles proves, in the end, to be less than fully satisfying. Liberal modernity addresses itself only to the animal in man, and the soul soon begins to hunger for a nourishment that modernity cannot provide. Such societies offer enlightened self-interest in the service of the desires of the body. Such a life contains nothing that could compel our admiration, nothing capable of satisfying the deeper, though less immediately felt, longings of reason for moral nobility and philosophical insight. As religion has progressively lost its grip on our imagination, and hence its ability to ennoble even our most ordinary activities, the crassness of our civilization has appeared with ever greater clarity. Unable to change our nature, we cannot in the end conceal from ourselves the lowness and banality of such a way of life.

Confronted with the prospect of life in such a society, the young—more awake to the promptings of nature, perhaps because they are not yet fully formed in the dominant opinions of their culture—react as the youthful Glaucon reacts, in Book II of the *Republic*, to what he calls the "city of sows," the city dedicated exclusively to the needs of the body. There must be more to life than this, they think. And of course they are right. But since they have not received the classical rearing in music that draws out the soul's natural attraction to the virtues of character and mind, they can have no accurate sense of what that more is. Hence, they turn to the most obvious thing: overindulgence of the pleasures of the body. Bored with liberal modernity's sober and cautious pursuit of pleasure, they turn instead to the careless and even reckless enjoyment of excessive pleasure, as well as to the music that celebrates and encourages such enjoyment as a way of life. Bloom is essentially correct that a certain kind of rock—at least the most daring rock of his time, to which he was responding—is primarily about sex, infantile sex pursued to extremes purely for the sake of its own physical pleasure.

This is not, however, the last stage of the youthful soul's, or of rock's, progress under conditions of liberal modernity. Sexual overindulgence proves in the end no more responsive to our most human desires than the timid bourgeois pleasure seeking from which the soul recoiled in the first place. The insufficiency of such excessive sexual gratification, moreover, is more keenly sensed by those who have grown up with it, to whom it was never forbidden and for whom it therefore has no happy association with the previous liberation from irksome restraints. Thus the members of Generation X show more awareness of the inadequacy of hedonistic sex as the end of life than their baby boomer parents.

Once again the young seek for more, but once again, in the absence of proper musical education, they have no idea where to look. They have exhausted the body as a source of fulfillment, but they know nothing of reason. Hence, they turn from bodily appetite to the far more interesting and dangerous regions of what the *Republic* calls the spirited part of the soul, the seat of anger and self-assertion. The satisfactions of spiritedness, at least in their coarser forms, are easily accessible. They require no refining education of the soul through orderly and graceful music. Indeed, the spirited satisfactions of which our ill-educated youth are capable do not even require the abandonment of excessive sexual gratification—which is convenient, as such habits are not easily cast aside. Certain spirited pleasures can be added to the indulgence of the body, and this solution appears, at least initially, responsive to the longing of the soul for more than the dominant culture has to offer. After all, that sexual excess alone is not fully satisfying need not mean that it is to be dispensed with, only supplemented.

Hence, the emergence, as we noted in chapter one, of a new, more disturbing popular music, one that adds violence to sex and is dually obscene for its celebration of both unrestrained physical gratification and the joys of uncontrolled spirited self-assertion. Indeed, the apparent summit of the new rock and rap's perverse genius is not merely to add spiritedness to sex but actually to combine the two: intercourse itself is presented not only as a source of physical pleasure but also as an occasion for self-assertion, as a handy means of gratifying the body with the aid of another while simultaneously gratifying the spirited element by degrading the other.

This is a phenomena of which Bloom, with his emphasis on rock as the music of sexual desire, seems unaware, perhaps because it had not yet reached full fruition. *The Closing of the American Mind* was written and published in the mid-1980s, and it seems that only in the 1990s has violent rage taken its place as the equal of sexual self-indulgence among the themes of popular music. To be sure, Bloom, by including "hate" as well as "sex" as one of rock's "great lyrical themes," displays some awareness of rock's spirited inclinations. Yet in Bloom's account, as well as in the music of which he wrote, such manifestations of spiritedness are merely epiphenomenal, derivative of rock's more fundamental concern with infantile sexuality. Rock's "hate" is for Bloom ultimately in the service of sex, merely an indignant response to those social and familial authorities seeking to impose limits on sexual gratification.[41] In the most recent controversial rock and rap, however, the pleasures of the spirited part of the soul are elevated to an equality with sex, and anger is embraced for its own sake and not merely as a defender of the rights of the body. Indeed, how except on this analysis could the "rage" of pop music persist and even flourish over the last decade and a half, during which time the efforts of social and familial authorities to impose sexual moderation on the young have faded and all but disappeared? Today government hands out free condoms to schoolchildren with minimal protest from parents, who are for the most part resigned to, if not supportive of, their children's promiscuity. Pop music's turn to spiritedness as itself a source of satisfaction appears clearly in the fact that its rage is now directed not against those who seek to take sexual pleasure away—they no longer exist—but instead against the partner who willingly provides it.

No doubt those more favorably disposed toward such popular music will, falling back on the idea of art as passionate political protest, contend that it represents not a barbaric celebration of spirited self-assertion for its own sake but instead the proper mobilization of spiritedness in opposition to injustice. While such an interpretation might plausibly explain some violent rap songs directed against the representatives of what the black musicians take to be oppressive political authority, it cannot explain rap's frequently expressed hostility toward women. Nor can it account for the equally violent and misogynistic character of much hard rock, primarily produced by the white children of the middle class. Nor can it explain the popularity of both violent rap and hard rock with the white teenagers of affluent suburbia, who are the primary market for such music,[42] but who have not only not been oppressed but have in fact had every material satisfaction one could desire. Such people turn to violent, excessively spirited pop not out of a sense of injustice but as a more interesting alternative to the banality of the life of bodily gratification alone.

On this analysis, our sexually and violently obscene popular music appears as an increasingly unwholesome but nonetheless understandable reaction on the part of the young to the spiritual poverty of liberal modernity. And as an alternative to its thrilling barbarism the critics of such music offer nothing but more of the soullessness of liberal modernity's cautious and calculating hedonism.

In this light we can appreciate the irony of the complaint of one of the more prominent critics of contemporary rap music: "Why can't rap songs talk about a black man going to work downtown in his three-piece suit?"[43] Such a life, the life of a businessman, is inherently prosaic and thus does not lend itself, unlike the glitz of savagery or the noble grandeur of classical virtue, to a musical presentation. Violent rap and rock could only emerge and become popular because the young some time ago saw through the amusical shallowness of liberal modernity's "good life" yet were morally and intellectually unprepared to seek the truly good life.

Of course, the ancient political philosophers could easily diagnose our sickness. Plato's *Republic* contains an account of the degeneration of regimes that reads in part like a history of modern America: The amusical oligarchic man, who appreciates virtue not for its beauty but only as a means to the satisfaction of desire and who therefore pursues pleasure soberly and prudently, is succeeded by the democratic man, who pursues pleasure carelessly and to excess and who is, in turn, finally succeeded by the tyrannical man, whose soul is dominated by a strange combination of excessive desire and excessive spiritedness: he is a slave to his desiring part, and yet, recognizing the unhappiness of his way of life, hates himself for it. Whether or not he foresaw its possibility, Plato would no doubt appreciate the attraction of a music, like ours, that allows such a soul to perfect its tyranny by simultaneously increasing its slavery to desire while projecting its self-loathing onto others.

The ancients could also prescribe a cure for our pathologies of the soul: the serious attempt, including the educational use of the right kind of music, to encourage our pursuit of the highest goods attainable by man, reason's enjoyment of moral nobility and theoretical truth. This, of course, is a daunting prospect in light of the discipline it necessarily imposes on the desires, which are, as even the ancients admit, the biggest and strongest part of the soul and therefore inclined to resist such a project. We can look with sympathy on the early modern temptation to dispense with the pursuit of human excellence and instead to erect society on a basis apparently more reliable because more agreeable to desire: the promotion only of peace and prosperity, the conditions of comfortable self-preservation. Yet, as our argument indicates, early modernity cannot in the long run attain even the humble goal it sets for itself: instead the society it creates eventually gives rise, as we are currently witnessing, to irrational and unruly passions that threaten the domestic peace and security the early moderns set out to achieve. Hence it seems necessary to strive for the highest things identified by the ancients, from which striving the decent things for which the early moderns hope may emerge as a by-product. To put it another way, and to borrow a phrase from C. S. Lewis, it appears that civilization can only be preserved by people who care about something higher than civilization.

In the realm of action no less than in the realm of thought, in politics no less than in philosophy, liberal modernity, which is base, gives rise to and is powerless to resist illiberal modernity, which is barbaric. Just as the hedonistic and amusical political philosophy of Hobbes, Locke, and Montesquieu gave rise to the excessively spirited musical reaction of Rousseau and Nietzsche, so in the life of our own civilization has the hedonistic social life based on the teaching of the early moderns given rise to uncontrolled spirited passions that find their expression in, and are in turn stoked by, the barbaric music with which we are confronted. In both its amusical account of man and in the amusical education it provides the young, liberal modernity dethrones reason and starves the spirit, which could have found its proper and moderate satisfaction in serving reason's rule in the soul. It all but guarantees that when spiritedness breaks free and seeks the nourishment it has been denied, it will rage uncontrolled by rational limits, that it will manifest itself—as it does in the popular music that has rightly disturbed so many—as implacable self-assertion.

The solution to our musical and moral difficulties, as we have suggested, is at hand: the musical political philosophy of the ancients that, by enthroning reason in the soul, harmonizes the whole soul and provides for its truest happiness. Our relief at the presence of a solution, however, is tempered by our recognition of its costliness. As we have seen, music's ability to harmonize the soul is intelligible and plausible only in light of the classical assertion of the centrality of reason in human nature, the rational order of the cosmos, and reason's natural attraction to that order and desire to make it present in our thought and action. Yet such beliefs are not widely held today; and where they are professed, they do not seem to be taken with great seriousness. Our embrace of the ancient solution would require a radical transformation in our understanding of what we are, what the universe is, and how we are related to it. The necessity of such a transformation is clear. Whether we are capable of it, or even willing to try, remains to be seen.

Notes

1 *Cultural Dissonance*

1 Ressner 1991, 17.
2 See Medved 1992.
3 Leo 1990b, 15.
4 Dahir 1995, 60-62.
5 Pattison 1987, 177-78, 185.
6 Linton 1999, 12. Linton's intention in the article is by no means to give aid and comfort to the defenders of porn rock. It is rather to refute the claims of Don Campbell, popularizer of the supposed intellectual, emotional, and physical benefits of the music of Mozart. Nevertheless, as Linton's remark about the error of the moralistic critics of the Rolling Stones indicates, his argument lends support to those who defend such music on the grounds that it has no serious impact on how people behave.
7 Ehrenreich 1992, 89; Cocks 1985.
8 DeCurtis and Light 1991, 32.
9 Ehrenreich 1992, 89.
10 Quoted in Kinsley 1992, 88.
11 Bloom 1987a, 75, 79, 78.
12 Ibid., 79.
13 Ibid., 79, 72.
14 Ibid., 73, 81.
15 Pattison 1987, viii-ix.
16 Ibid., 5, 6, 7.
17 Ibid., 48, 95 (emphasis in original), 58, 58-59.

18 Ibid., 128, 169, 93.
19 Ibid., 102, 95, 74.
20 Ibid., 210.
21 Ibid., 210, 27-28.
22 Strauss 1959, 10.

2 Plato's Music of the Soul

1   Unless otherwise indicated, all quotations in this chapter are from Book
    III of the *Republic*, where the main body of Plato's account of music is
    found. I have used Allan Bloom's translation. References to other parts
    of Plato's works make use of the Stephanus numbers, and references to
    passages in the *Republic* outside Book III are abbreviated *Rep.*
2   It might be objected at the outset that we can in fact learn little or noth-
    ing from the *Republic's* treatment of rhythm and harmony because we
    know too little about how the music of which it speaks sounded. Never-
    theless, I believe it is possible to understand to a considerable extent what
    Socrates is talking about. As we will see, the standards in light of which
    he evaluates music, such as simplicity and grace, are readily intelligible
    to us.
3   *Rep.* 375b1-2.
4   *Rep.* 375e-376c.
5   West writes: "'Harmonics,' in ancient terminology, is the science of deal-
    ing with the ordered arrangement of notes in scales and the relationships
    between scales. It was not concerned like modern harmonic theory with
    chords and chord successions" (1992, 5 n.7).
6   Bloom 1968, 453.
7   *Rep.* 379c4-5
8   Those familiar with modern music theory should not be misled by the
    fact that the names by which Socrates and Glaucon refer to the particu-
    lar modes are the same as those applied to contemporary modal scales.
    The contemporary modes—Ionian, Dorian, Phrygian, Lydian, Mixo-
    lydian, Aeolian, and Locrian—are based on the medieval church modes,
    which took the names, but not the actual structures, of the ancient Greek
    modes. See West 1992, 186 n.100.
9   The harp, typically possessing nine to twenty strings, was literally many-
    stringed, while the lute, having only four to five, was effectively so: like the
    modern guitar, the lute's strings were able to be stopped against the neck
    of the instrument to shorten the vibrating length and thus raise the pitch.
    See West 1992, 73, 80.
10 Anderson 1966, 8; West 1992, 84. In light of its structure, West is critical

of the common translation of aulos as "flute" and suggests "pipe" or "shawm" instead (1992, 1, 85).

11 Socrates also says that the city will include a sort of pipe for the country herdsmen. The fact that he confines the pipe's use to a class for whom no education is outlined in the *Republic*, however, indicates that it would, unlike the lyre and cither, serve no educational function.

12 Anderson 1980a, 503.

13 Mercatante 1988, 579.

14 Bloom 1968, 453.

15 See Bloom 1968, 453.

16 On the definition of this Greek term, see Bloom 1968, 454 n.52.

17 *Rep.* 377a10-b3.

18 *Rep.* 601b1, 401d6-9.

19 *Laws* 812c.

20 It is perhaps worth noting in this context that the order presented by rhythm and harmony is perceived as something apart from the actual physical sensations involved in hearing. People can identify tunes even when they are played at a different tempo or in a different key, which suggests that they "do not remember simple melodies in terms of precise pitches and durations but in terms of patterns and relationships," which in turn demonstrates that musical memory involves "an abstraction from the physical stimulus" (Sloboda 1985, 4-5).

21 *Rep.* 560d-561d.

22 *Rep.* 601a-b.

23 *Rep.* 402d8-402e1.

24 *Rep.* 402a1.

25 *Rep.* 396d6-7.

26 *Rep.* 554d-e.

27 *Rep.* 424c3-6.

28 *Rep.* 373d8-e2, 586a7-b3.

29 *Rep.* 425a-d.

30 *Rep.* 425e-426a.

31 *Rep.* 389e1-2.

32 *Rep.* 431a-442d.

33 *Rep.* 442a6.

34 For the contrary argument that the education of the guardians renders them unfit for philosophic activity, see Steinberger 1989, 1220. For an account which, like mine, stresses the compatibility of the guardians' early education with the later philosophic education, see Barker 1964, 228-29.

35 *Rep.* 498b3-6, 571d-572a, 573e-574a.

36 *Rep.* 519a6-b6. See also Dobbs, who suggests that Glaucon's "inflamed and

limitless desires" must be purged to uncover the "original" and "unperverted" philosophic nature of *eros*, a "quickening of the soul responsive to evidence of the beauty of the cosmic order" (1994, 268).

37 *Rep.* 486d.

38 *Rep.* 500c-d.

39 On this connection between the orderly impression conveyed by the art of the city in speech and the order of the cosmos, see also Nettleship, who writes that for Plato "the laws of proportion, which are the condition of the beauty of art, seemed to betoken the presence of the same mind as is revealed in the immutable order of the universe" (1968, 69).

40 *Rep.* 359c4-5, 360b7-8, 419a1-3.

41 *Rep.* 466b7, 606d5-7, 444d-445b.

42 *Rep.* 575a4, 573e5, 578a7-12.

43 *Rep.* 580e-581b.

44 *Rep.* 505l0-e1, 611b8-612a3.

45 *Rep.* 617b4-6 (my emphasis), 532a1-b3.

3 *Aristotle's Musical Education*

1 My analysis of Book 8 omits consideration of the last eighteen lines of Chapter 7, which most scholars agree are an interpolation. See Anderson 1966, 140, 145; Lord 1982, 147.

2 Unless otherwise indicated, all quotations in this chapter are from Book 8 of the *Politics*. I have used the translation of Carnes Lord. References to other passages in Aristotle will identify the title of the work and make use of the Bekker numbers.

3 *Politics* 1252b30, 1280b39-1281a5. In subsequent references the *Politics* will be abbreviated *Pol.*

4 *Nicomachean Ethics* 1103a17. In subsequent references the *Nicomachean Ethics* will be abbreviated *N.E.*

5 *N.E.* 1099b30-35.

6 *Pol.* 1336b28-35.

7 *N.E.* 1097b22-1098a20.

8 This is not to say that the education in gymnastic has no effect on character at all. Instead, Aristotle's treatment suggests that such education in the proper doses is beneficial to the body but that when it is taken to an extreme it results in a savage character. This is the effect sought and achieved by the Spartans, which they mistakenly take to be courage.

9 Lord 1984, 269-270 n. 14, 269 n. 11.

10 See also Anderson, who contends that Aristotle uses the term "music" in a sense that is equivalent to the contemporary English understanding and that he "attenuate[s]" the older Greek concept of "*mousike*, in which music

and literature were joined together" (1980b, 588). In contrast, see Lord 1982, 85-87.

11 In quoting from the *Poetics* I have generally followed the Loeb Classical Library translation by W. Hamilton Fyfe, but I have rendered the translation more literal in some instances. Fyfe consistently renders the Greek *harmonia* as "tune" rather than the more obvious "harmony."

12 *Poetics* 1447a-b.

13 Anderson presents Aristotle's argument here as an attempt to refute Plato's supposed denial of the ethical power of instrumental music (1966, 126). But to suggest that Plato would deny this contradicts the *Republic's* affirmation of the ability of rhythm and harmony most powerfully to lay hold of the soul and bring into it grace or gracelessness. See also Lord 1982, 212 n. 22.

14 *Pol.* 1336b12-17, 1340a35-38, and *Poetics* 1448a.

15 *Pol.* 1331a9-14 and 1330b27-31.

16 *Rep.* 401c6-d3.

17 Here the disagreement between Aristotle and Plato involves not music's power nor the proper ends with which to use it but instead the particular effect of a particular mode.

18 *N.E.* 1104a13-27, 1108b10-15.

19 *Pol.* 1295a34-37.

20 *N.E.* 1104b19-27, 1106b15-23.

21 My emphasis.

22 *N.E.* 1103b1-3.

23 *N.E.* 1179b23-30.

24 *Pol.* 1331b26-28.

25 *N.E.* 1141b8-14. Lord (1982) and Nichols (1992) both offer accounts of how Aristotle's music education contributes to prudence. Their accounts differ from mine, however, by focusing on music in the sense of poetry and drama and ignoring the contribution made to prudence by Aristotle's education in tune and rhythm.

26 *N.E.* 1140b12-20. Aristotle defines passions as "generally those states of consciousness which are accompanied by pleasure and pain" (*N.E.* 1105b19-24).

27 *N.E.* 1147a11-18.

28 *N.E.* 1099a17-22, 1099a10-17, 1148b15-20, 1173b21-26, 1113a30-36.

29 *N.E.* 1117b1-9, 1119a1-6.

30 *N.E.* 1119b5-8.

31 *N.E.* 1177a12-17.

32 For the contrary interpretation, that Aristotle does not believe in the ability of rhythm and tune to "contribute to intellectual well-being," see Anderson 1966, 136. Lindsay implicitly advances the same position when

he claims that "the highest purpose" of music "is to foster ethical virtue" (1991, 506).

33 *N.E.* 1177b5-15.

34 *Pol.* 1334b14-16.

35 *N.E.* 1103a14-19, *Pol.* 1332b9-10.

36 *N.E.* 1154b21-26.

37 *N.E.* 1141a1-5.

38 *Pol.* 1254a21-34.

39 *N.E.* 1118a1-23.

40 On this issue see also Swanson, who points out that Aristotle's admonition that citizens should not enjoy music in the same way as children, slaves, and some animals leads us "to the notion that music affects the soul by engaging thought" (1992, 153).

41 *Poetics*, 1448b.

42 *Poetics*, 1459a.

43 *N.E.* 1104a13-15. For a different account of the connection between music and philosophy in Book 8, see Lindsay, who points out that Aristotle's claim at 1342a28-32 that the best city must use harmonies approved by those participating in philosophy suggests a ruling role for philosophy similar to that advocated in the *Republic* (1991, 506-507).

44 *Pol.* 1310a13-23.

45 *Pol.* 1310a23-35.

46 See also Jaffa 1975, 67.

47 *Pol.* 1258a2-4.

48 *N.E.* 1121b32-1122a3, my emphasis.

49 *Rhetoric* 1368b19 and 1381a30-31.

50 *Pol.* 1305a36-38 and 1308a4-9.

51 *Pol.* 1304b21-22 and 1305a3-8.

4   An Amusical Interlude

1 Montesquieu 1989, 39-41.

2 Ibid. (my emphasis).

3 Strauss 1959, 40.

4 Machiavelli 1980, 93.

5 Ibid., 17-18.

6 *Rep.* 359c. On the issues discussed in this paragraph see Strauss, who writes that, while the ancient teaching "was based on the assumption that morality is something substantial: that it is a force in the soul of man," Machiavelli rejects this view, claiming instead that "[m]an is not by nature directed toward virtue" (1959, 42).

7 Hobbes 1991, 53, 33, 39.

8 Ibid., 26. On this point see Strauss, who contends that Hobbes believed in the "unintelligible character of the universe" (1953, 174).

9 Hobbes 1991, 70.

10 Quoted in Strauss 1953, 166.

11 Ibid., 231; see also 9, 117.

12 Ibid., 9.

13 Ibid., 111.

14 Rahe 1994, 148.

15 Ibid., 131-32. Here again Hobbes appears to be following Machiavelli's lead. Strauss writes that Machiavelli can be presented as arguing that "justice" can be secured not by "formation of character and moral appeal" but by "making injustice utterly unprofitable," that is, by "the right kind of institutions: institutions with teeth in them" (1959, 43).

16 Locke 1960, 328.

17 Quoted in Strauss 1953, 247.

18 Strauss 1959, 214.

19 Locke 1960, 374-75, 316, 312.

20 Ibid., 308. See also Goldwin, who points out that the "little Locke says of education in the *Two Treatises* has nothing to do with developing a sense of public duty; education is spoken of as having no purpose loftier than preparing children to take care of themselves" (1987, 508-509).

21 See Strauss 1953, 233

22 Montesquieu 1989, 6-7.

23 Ibid., 5-8.

24 Ibid., 156, 168, 157.

25 Ibid., 24-25.

26 Ibid., 155, 157.

27 Strauss 1959, 50.

5 *Rousseau's Music of Passionate Patriotism*

1 O'Dea 1995, 7, 219 n. 31.

2 Wokler 1995, 1.

3 Unless otherwise indicated, all quotations in this chapter are from Rousseau's *Essay on the Origin of Languages*. The version referred to is that found in *On the Origin of Language*, translated and edited by John H. Moran and Alexander Gode (1966).

4 It is clear that Rousseau means by "melody" what Plato and Aristotle mean by rhythm and harmony. Rousseau indicates that rhythm is an essential part of melody, and (like Plato and Aristotle) even that it is by itself imi-

tative of the passions (1975, 346). Moreover, he repeatedly claims that melody imitates the "accents" of passionate speech, and by "accents" he means variations of pitch.

5   On this point see Arthur Melzer, who contends that for Rousseau "[t]he goal of politics is not merely to secure preservation and wealth, but to produce virtuous, healthy human beings" (1983b, 633). See also Leo Strauss's observation that for Rousseau modern people are lower than the ancients because the former "lack the public spirit or the patriotism" of the latter (1953, 253). See also Allan Bloom, who claims that for Rousseau the modern state is defective because it seeks to secure only the conditions of happiness and not happiness itself (1987b, 559-560).

6   Rousseau 1964, 51.

7   Rousseau 1960, 132-133; 1964, 43; Shklar 1969, 13; Strauss 1953, 253.

8   For a good discussion of the similarities and differences between Plato's and Rousseau's teachings on the politics of music see Kelly, who aptly observes that, "[w]hereas Plato is interested in taming the power of music and submitting it to reason, Rousseau is interested in taking advantage of the untamed power of melody" (1997, 29-30). Thus we see that Rousseau's approach to music confirms Strauss's observation that Rousseau's thought represents an apparent return to the ancients insofar as it focuses on virtue, but an advance of modernity insofar as it denigrates reason and exalts passion to a degree unheard of among the early moderns (Strauss 1953, 252).

9   Rousseau suggests the possibility of such a misunderstanding when he claims that "we have no idea of sonorous and harmonious language, spoken as much according to sounds as it is according to words."

10   Incidentally, Rousseau follows Plato and Aristotle in attributing greater emotional power to music than to the visual arts. See his article on opera in his *Complete Dictionary of Music* (1975, 298).

11   *Essay* 57. The tendency of Rousseau's thought toward a belief in the natural status of melody is also recognized by Wokler (1995, 108) and Gourevitch (1993). The latter writes that Rousseau's argument in the *Essay* points to the existence of a "'natural' human language, or 'natural' recognition of 'natural' signs," specifically a "natural prosody of the passions ... their characteristic accents" (1993, 24). In contrast, O'Dea claims that in the *Essay* Rousseau holds that "music is a cultural rather than a natural phenomenon" and "rejects natural status for melody" (1995, 73, 79). On the other hand, he admits that an anecdote related elsewhere by Rousseau about seeing an Armenian moved by an Italian aria implies a natural status for melody and a universality of the passions it expresses (1995, 30). Scott (1995) also sees some natural basis for musical communication, but he tends to stress cultural variability much more.

12 Rousseau 1964, 95, 135. This view is held by Melzer (1983b, 637), who writes that for Rousseau "men are by nature asocial and selfish," and by Kelly (1987, 329), who argues that natural humans are unable to appreciate imitative music because they are "immune to moral impressions."

13 Ibid., 95, 133.

14 Indeed, the passions of the heart seem to be based upon pity. See Masters 1968, 49, and Kelly 1997, 26.

15 Rousseau 1964, 104.

16 Ibid., 142-151. It is in this light that we can understand Rousseau's modification, in the *Second Discourse*, of his initial harsh assessment of man's move into society. At the outset he claims that "[i]n becoming sociable," man simply degenerates (1964, 111). Only later, in light of the revelation that savage society, and not man's original state, is "the veritable prime of the world," does it become clear that not progress itself but only progress "subsequent" to savage society is movement "toward the decrepitude of the species" (1964, 150).

17 Ibid., 150.

18 Ibid., 92.

19 On this point see also Gourevitch 1993, 28.

20 Rousseau 1960, 47.

21 Rousseau 1964, 78.

22 Ibid., 39-41.

23 Christopher Kelly similarly observes that Rousseau's analysis of language in the *Essay* "builds upon and confirms the argument of the *First Discourse*, in which Rousseau insists upon the negative effects of direct intrusion of philosophy into public life" (1987, 332).

24 Rousseau 1964, 95.

25 Ibid., 116.

26 It might be objected that Rousseau follows the ancient understanding, since they also held that knowing is undertaken with a view to enjoyment of pleasure. The difference, of course, is that the ancients believed there was a pleasure to be found in the activity of knowing itself, whereas here Rousseau is suggesting that knowledge is pursued to facilitate pleasures unconnected to knowing. On this point see also Kelly 1997, 35-36.

27 Rousseau 1964, 42.

28 O'Dea also views the teaching of the *Essay* as one of unequivocal pessimism (1995, 55). See also Arthur Melzer, who argues that for Rousseau "civilized decadence is irreversible" (1983a, 303).

29 Wokler 1995, 23.

30 Rousseau 1975, 338, 160-162.

31 O'Dea 1995, 53.

32 Quoted in Scott 1995, 13.

33 Scott 1995, 13.

6 *Nietzsche's Tragic Politics of Music*

1 See Jones 1994, 14-15.
2 Quoted in Hayman 1980, 145.
3 In light of Nietzsche's later criticism of *The Birth of Tragedy* and disillusionment with Wagner, one might doubt that this work represents his mature views on music and politics. Nevertheless, the "Attempt at a Self-Criticism" with which Nietzsche introduces the later edition of *The Birth of Tragedy* indicates that he repudiates not the notion that there can be a culture-shaping music but his belief that German music generally, and Wagner's in particular, was a modern version of such music.
4 Unless otherwise noted, all quotations in this chapter are from *The Birth of Tragedy*. The version referred to is that found in *The Basic Writings of Nietzsche*, translated and edited by Walter Kaufmann (1968a). Unless otherwise indicated, emphases are Nietzsche's.
5 Nietzsche 1990, 292.
6 Quoted in Hayman 1980, 145.
7 Nietzsche 1990, 293.
8 Quoted in Hayman 1980, 97 (my emphasis).
9 My emphasis.
10 My argument here agrees more with that of Detwiler (1990, 145), who claims that in *The Birth of Tragedy* Dionysian art "is presented as a genuine source of transcendent metaphysical insight," than with that of Thiele (1990, 123-124), who is inclined to view tragedy more as a celebration of "illusion over reality, the appearance of truth . . . over truth." See also Copleston (1963, 397-8), who interprets *The Birth of Tragedy* as teaching that Dionysian art, far from veiling reality, actually "triumphantly affirm[s] and embrace[s] existence in all its darkness and horror."
11 For a similar account of musical tragedy as the closest approximation of truth that we can stand, see Dannhauser (1974, 121).
12 On Nietzsche's understanding of Socrates and Plato as Apollinians, see Dannhauser (1974, 62, 128).

7 *Music and Passion*

1 Weinberger 1998.
2 Ibid.
3 See Strunk 1950, 64-68, 73-74, 80, 93.
4 Weinberger 1998; Coplan 1997; Shreeve 1996.
5 Shreeve 1996.

6 Gregory 1997,124; also see Shreeve 1996.
7 Weinberger 1998.
8 Ibid.
9 Ibid.
10 Hepper 1991.
11 Bower 1996, 151.
12 Ibid.
13 West 1992, 158-159, 177.
14 Strunk 1950, 382, 413, 600.
15 Ibid., 802-03, 849, 861.
16 Westley and Gidense 1998, 103.
17 Shreeve 1996.
18 Crozier 1997, 75.
19 Hargreaves and North 1997, 1.
20 Kaemmer 1993, 45.
21 Merriam 1964, 219.
22 Quoted in Merriam 1964, 219.
23 Kaemmer 1993, 134.
24 Rouget 1985, 316.
25 Ibid., 91.
26 Kaemmer 1993, 61-62.
27 West 1992, 31.
28 Ibid.
29 Kaemmer 1993, 62.
30 Linton 1999, 11.
31 See Courtright et al. 1990, and Ragneskog et al. 1996.
32 Crozier 1997, 80-81.
33 Ibid.
34 Ibid., 76.
35 Coplan 1997.
36 Kaemmer 1993, 159.
37 Ibid., 148, 157.
38 Quoted in Kaemmer 1993, 47.
39 Ibid., 156.
40 Ibid., 208.
41 *Rep.* 424c-d.
42 Rahe 1994a, 113.
43 See, for example, Grandin et al. 1998.
44 See the popular account of these issues in Begley 1996.
45 Minsky 1982, 25.
46 Sloboda 1985, 263-265.
47 See Glausuisz 1997, 28.

48 See Shreeve 1996.
49 See Weinberger 1998.
50 Grandin et al. 1998.
51 Rauscher et al. 1993, 611.
52 *Science News* 1994, 143. Other scientists have achieved similar results. See, for example, Grandin et al. 1998.
53 See Shreeve 1996.
54 I am grateful to Professor Larry Arnhart for calling this difficulty to my attention.
55 This is the expression used by Leo Strauss to describe the tradition of thought initiated by Hobbes. See Strauss 1953, 169.
56 Quoted in Rahe 1994b, 123.
57 For a lucid and detailed account of the Founders' intellectual debt to the early modern political philosophers, see Rahe 1994b.
58 Hamilton, Madison, and Jay 1961, 61.
59 Ibid., 51-52 and 349.
60 Will 1983, 18, 13, 143.
61 Lerner 1996, 3.
62 Machiavelli 1980, 93.
63 *Rep.* 440c-d.
64 *Pol.* 1325a30-1325b10.
65 Kelly 1987, 332.
66 Rousseau 1964, 148-149.
67 Nietzsche 1968b, 293.

8   Hungry Souls

1   *Pol.* 1341b25-30.
2   *Rep.* 402b-c.
3   Pattison 1987, 36.
4   Ibid., 27.
5   Ibid., 182.
6   Ibid., 27.
7   Ibid.
8   Ibid., 211.
9   Ibid., 28.
10   Ibid., 211.
11   Ibid., 58.
12   Ibid.
13   Bloom 1987, 71.
14   Ibid., 72.
15   Ibid.

16 Bloom 1989, 239.

17 Bloom 1987, 71 (Bloom's emphasis).

18 Crockett 1989, 254.

19 Zappa 1989, 248.

20 Weisberg 1987.

21 Greider 1989, 245.

22 Menand 1987.

23 Bloom 1987, 79.

24 Ibid., 270.

25 Ibid., 60.

26 Ibid., 277.

27 Zucchino 1985, 16-17.

28 See DeCurtis and Light 1991, Medved 1992, and Brownback 1998.

29 Pattison is well aware of this (1987, 137).

30 Linton 1999, 10.

31 Ibid., 11.

32 Ibid.

33 Ibid., 12.

34 Ibid., 12-13.

35 Pattison 1987, 177-78. See also 185.

36 This is not to say that serious people do not engage in play. On Aristotle's teaching, play is needed by all people as a kind of rest from exertion. Serious people, however, do not consume all of their leisure time merely recovering from exertion but use as much as they can for serious study and reflection. But even from such exertions of the mind some rest is no doubt needed in the form of play.

37 *Rep.* 378d-e.

38 *Rep.* 395c-d.

39 *Rep.* 392c-394a.

40 *N.E.* 1180a30-35.

41 See Bloom 1987, 74.

42 See Medved 1992, 47.

43 Quoted in Chappell 1995.

Bibliography

Aldridge, D., and G. Aldridge. 1992. "Two Epistemologies: Music Therapy and Medicine in the Treatment of Dementia." *The Arts in Psychotherapy* 19: 243-255.

Allman, William F. 1990. "The Musical Brain: Studies of Pitch and Melody Reveal the Inner Workings of the Mind, from Basic Perception to Appreciating Beauty." *U.S. News and World Report*, 11 June, 56.

Anderson, Warren D. 1966. *Ethos and Education in Greek Music*. Cambridge: Harvard University Press.

————. 1980a. "Apollo." In *The New Grove Dictionary of Music and Musicians*, vol. 1, ed. by Stanley Sadie. London: Macmillan Publishing Limited.

————. 1980b. "Aristotle." In *The New Grove Dictionary of Music and Musicians*, vol. 1, ed. by Stanley Sadie. London: Macmillan Publishing Limited.

Aristotle. 1960. *The Poetics*, trans. by W. Hamilton Fyfe. Cambridge: Harvard University Press.

————. 1961. *Problems*, trans. by W. S. Hett. Cambridge: Harvard University Press.

————. 1984. *The Politics*, trans. by Carnes Lord. Chicago: University of Chicago Press.

————. 1990. *Nicomachean Ethics*, trans. by H. Rackham. Cambridge: Harvard University Press.

———. 1991. *The Art of Rhetoric*, trans. by J.H. Freese. Cambridge: Harvard University Press.

Barker, Ernest. 1959. *The Political Thought of Plato and Aristotle*. New York: Dover Publishers.

———. 1964. *Greek Political Theory: Plato and his Predecessors*. N.P.: Methuen and Co., Ltd.

Begley, Sharon. 1996. "Your Child's Brain." *Newsweek*, 19 February, 54.

Bloom, Allan. 1968. Notes and Interpretive Essay. In *The Republic of Plato*, trans. by Allan Bloom. New York: Basic Books.

———. 1987a. *The Closing of the American Mind*. New York: Simon and Schuster.

———. 1987b. "Jean-Jacques Rousseau." In *History of Political Philosophy*, third edition, ed. by Leo Strauss and Joseph Cropsey. Chicago: University of Chicago Press, 559-580.

———. 1989. "Too Much Tolerance." In *Essays on* The Closing of the American Mind, ed. By Robert L. Stone. Chicago: Chicago Review Press, 239.

Boehlert, Eric. 1997a. "Manson Mania." *Rolling Stone*, 12 June, 27.

———. 1997b. "Meet the New Boss." *Rolling Stone*, 10-24 July, 30.

———. 1997c. "Culture Skirmishes." *Rolling Stone*, 21 August, 29.

Bower, Bruce. 1996. "Infants Tune Up to Music's Core Qualities." *Science News*, 7 September, 151.

Brownback, Sam. 1998. "The Melodies of Mayhem." *Policy Review*, November.

Chambers, Veronica. 1998. "Family Rappers." *Newsweek*, 19 January, 66.

Chappell, Kevin. 1995. "What's Wrong (and Right) about Black Music." *Ebony*, September, 25.

Cocks, Jay. 1985. "Rock is a Four-Letter Word: A Senate Committee Asks: Have Rock Lyrics Gone too Far?" *Time*, 30 September, 70.

Coplan, David. 1997. "Musics." *International Social Science Journal* 49:4 (December): 585.

Copleston, Frederick. 1963. *A History of Philosophy*, vol. 7. Westminster: The Newman Press.

—————. 1975. *Friedrich Nietzsche: Philosopher of Culture*. New York: Barnes and Noble Books.

Courtright, P., et al. 1990. "Dinner Music: Does it Affect The Behavior of Psychiatric Inpatients?" *Journal of Psychosocial Nursing* 28: 37-40.

Crockett, Steven. 1989. "Blam! Bam! Bloom! Boom!" In *Essays on* The Closing of the American Mind, ed. by Robert L. Stone. Chicago: Chicago Review Press, 253.

Crozier, W. Ray. 1997. "Music and Social Influence." In *The Social Psychology of Music*, ed. by David J. Hargreaves and Adrian C. North. Oxford: Oxford University Press.

Dahir, Mubarak S. 1995. "Sticker Shock." *Reason*, July, 60-62.

Dannhauser, Werner. 1974. *Nietzsche's View of Socrates*. Ithaca, N.Y.: Cornell University Press.

—————. 1987. "Friedrich Nietzsche." In *History of Political Philosophy*, third, edition, ed. by Leo Strauss and Joseph Cropsey. Chicago: University of Chicago Press, 829-50.

DeCurtis, Anthony. 1986. "Study Refutes PMRC Claim, Says Kids Don't Listen to Lyrics." *Rolling Stone*, 14 August, 11.

—————, and Alan Light. 1991. "Opinion." *Rolling Stone*, 19 September, 32.

Depew, David J. 1991. "Politics, Music, and Contemplation in Aristotle's Ideal State." In *A Companion to Aristotle's Politics*, ed. by David Keyt and Fred D. Miller, Jr. Oxford: Blackwell.

Detwiler, Bruce. 1990. *Nietzsche and the Politics of Aristocratic Radicalism*. Chicago: University of Chicago Press.

Dobbs, Darrell. 1994. "Choosing Justice: Socrates' Model City and the Practice of Dialectic." *American Political Science Review* 88: 263-277.

Donnelly, Sally B. 1992. "The Fire around the Ice." *Time*, 22 June, 66.

Dowling, W. Jay, and Dane L. Harwood. 1986. *Music Cognition*. New York: Academic Press, Inc.

Ehrenreich, Barbara. 1992. "Ice-T: Is the Issue Social Responsibility or is it Creative Freedom?" *Time*, 20 July, 89.

Elliott, Laura. 1995. "The Power of Music." *The Washingtonian*, December, 72.

Farley, Christopher. 1993. "The Dogg is Unleashed." *Time*, 13 December, 78.

———. 1996. "Reborn to be Wild: Christian Pop used to be Soporific." *Time*, 22 January, 62.

Feder, Bernard, and Elaine Feder. N.D. *The Expressive Arts Therapies.* Englewood Cliffs, N.J.: Prentice Hall, Inc.

Field, Tiffany, et al. 1998. "Music Shifts Frontal EEG in Depressed Adolescents." *Adolescence* 33, no. 129 (Spring): 109.

"Fighting Words." 1995. *The New Yorker*, 12 June, 36.

Frankena, William K. 1965. *Three Historical Philosophies of Education: Aristotle, Kant, Dewey.* Glenview, Ill.: Scott, Foresman, and Company.

Galston, William A. 1991. *Liberal Purposes.* Cambridge: Cambridge University Press.

Gardels, Nathan. 1995. "Does Rock Wreck Families?" *New Perspectives Quarterly*, Spring 1995, 31.

Glausuisz, Josie. 1997. "The Neural Orchestral." *Discover*, September, 28.

Goldwin, Robert A. 1987. "John Locke." In *History of Political Philosophy*, third edition, ed. by Leo Strauss and Joseph Cropsey. Chicago: University of Chicago Press, 476-511.

Gourevitch, Victor. 1993. "The Political Argument of Rousseau's *Essay on the Origin of Languages*." In *Pursuits of Reason: Essays in Honor of Stanley Cavell*, ed. by Ted Cohen, Paul Guyer, and Hilary Putnam. Lubbock: Texas Tech. University Press, 21-35.

Grandin, Temple, et al. 1998. "Spatial-Temporal Versus Language-Analytic Reasoning: The Role of Music Training." *Arts Education Policy Review* 99, no. 6 (July-August): 11.

Gregory, Andrew H. 1997. "The Roles of Music in Society: The Ethological Perspective." In *The Social Psychology of Music*, ed. by David J. Hargreaves and Adrian C. North. Oxford: Oxford University Press.

Greider, William. 1989. "Bloom and Doom." In *Essays on* The Closing of the American Mind, ed. By Robert L. Stone. Chicago: Chicago Review Press, 244.

Hamerlinck, John. 1995. "Killing Women: A Pop-Music Tradition?" *The Humanist*, July-August, 23.

Hamilton, Alexander, James Madison, and John Jay. 1961. *The Federalist*, ed. by Jacob Cooke. Middletown, Conn.: Wesleyan University Press.

Hampsher-Monk, Iain. 1992. *A History of Modern Political Thought: Major Political Thinkers from Hobbes to Marx*. Oxford: Blackwell.

Hargreaves, David J., and Adrian C. North. 1997. "The Social Psychology of Music." In *The Social Psychology of Music*, ed. by David J. Hargreaves and Adrian C. North. Oxford: Oxford University Press.

Hayman, Ronald. 1980. *Nietzsche: A Critical Life*. London: Weidenfeld and Nicolson.

Hepper, P. G. 1991. "An Examination of Fetal Learning Before and After Birth." *Irish Journal of Psychology* 12: 95-107.

Hitchens, Christopher. 1990. "Minority Report." *The Nation*, 30 July, 120.

Hobbes, Thomas. 1991. *Leviathan*, ed. by Richard Tuck. Cambridge: Cambridge University Press.

"Infants Tune in to the Sounds of Music." 1990. *Science News*, 21 July, 46.

Jaeger, Werner. 1943. *Paideia: The Ideals of Greek Culture*, vol. 2, trans. by Gilbert Highet. New York: Oxford University Press.

Jaffa, Harry V. 1975. *The Conditions of Freedom: Essays in Political Philosophy*. Baltimore: The Johns Hopkins University Press.

Jones, E. Michael. 1994. *Dionysos Rising: The Birth of Cultural Revolution out of the Spirit of Music*. San Francisco: Ignatius Press.

Jowett, B. 1885. Introduction. In *The Politics of Aristotle*, trans. by B. Jowett. Oxford: Clarendon Press.

Kaemmer, John E. 1993. *Music in Human Life: Anthropological Perspectives on Music*. Austin: University of Texas Press.

Kelly, Christopher. 1987. "To Persuade Without Convincing: The Language of Rousseau's Legislator." *American Journal of Political Science* 31: 321-335.

————. 1997. "Rousseau and the Case Against (and for) the Arts." In *The Legacy of Rousseau*, ed. by Clifford Orwin and Nathan Tarcov. Chicago: University of Chicago Press, 20-42.

Kendzierski, Lottie H. 1956. "Aristotle and Pagan Education." In *Some Philosophers on Education: Papers Concerning the Doctrines of Augustine, Aristotle, Aquinas, and Dewey*, ed. by Donald Gallagher. Milwaukee: Marquette University Press.

Kinnon, Joy Bennett. 1997. "Does Rap Have a Future? Will Gansta Rap Sink Hip-Hop?" *Ebony*, June, 76.

Kinsley, Michael. 1992. "Ice-T: Is the Issue Social Responsibility or is it Creative Freedom?" *Time*, 20 July, 88.

Lacayo, Richard. 1995. "Violent Reaction." *Time*, 12 June, 24.

"Landscapes and Lullabies." 1990. *U.S. News and World Report*, 11 June, 58.

Lang, Peter D. 1980. *Aristotle and the Problem of Moral Discernment*. Berne: Paul Schuchman.

"Learning Keys: Music May Give Kids' Minds a Head Start." *Prevention*, February, 24.

Leo, John. 1990a. "Polluting our Popular Culture." *U.S. News and World Report*, 2 July, 15.

————. 1990b. "Rock n' Roll's Hatemongering." *U.S. News and World Report*, 19 March, 17.

————. 1995. "The Leading Cultural Polluter." *U.S. News and World Report*, 27 March, 16.

Lerner, Michael. 1996. *The Politics of Meaning*. New York: Addison-Wesley Publishing Company.

Lindsay, Thomas K. 1991. "The 'God-Like Man' versus the 'Best Laws': Politics and Religion in Aristotle's *Politics*." *Review of Politics* 53: 488-509.

Linton, Michael. 1999. "The Mozart Effect." *First Things*, 91 (March): 10-13.

Locke, John. 1960. *Two Treatises of Government*. New York: New American Library.

Long, Cynthia. 1996. "Doctors Find Music Works Well with Sedatives and Anesthetics." *Insight on the News*, 23 December, 41.

Lord, Carnes. 1982. *Education and Culture in the Political Thought of Aristotle*. Ithaca, N.Y.: Cornell University Press.

————. 1984. Notes. In Aristotle's *The Politics*, trans. by Carnes Lord. Chicago: The University of Chicago Press.

Love, Robert. 1985a. "Furor over Rock Lyrics Intensifies." *Rolling Stone*, 12 September, 13.

————. 1985b. "Battle over Rock Lyrics Heads for Round Two." *Rolling Stone*, 26 September, 22.

Lowenthal, David. 1987. "Montesquieu." In *History of Political Philosophy*, third edition, ed. by Leo Strauss and Joseph Cropsey. Chicago: University of Chicago Press, 513-34.

Machiavelli, Niccolo. 1980. *The Prince*, trans. by Leo Paul S. de Alvarez. Prospect Heights, Ill.: Waveland Press.

Masters, Roger D. 1968. *The Political Philosophy of Rousseau*. Princeton: Princeton University Press.

McBee, Susan. 1985. "Now it's Labels on 'Porn Rock' to Protect Kids." *U.S. News and World Report*, 26 August, 52.

Medved, Michael. 1992. "The New Sound of Music." *The Public Interst*, Fall, 40-52.

Melzer, Arthur M. 1980. "Rousseau and the Problem of Bourgeois Society." *American Political Science Review* 74: 1018-1033.

———. 1983a. "Rousseau's 'Mission' and the Intention of His Writings." *American Journal of Political Science* 27: 294-320.

———. 1983b. "Rousseau's Moral Realism: Replacing Natural Law with the General Will." *American Political Science Review* 77: 633-651.

Menand, Louis. 1987. Review of *The Closing of the American Mind*. *The New Republic*, 25 May, 38.

Mercatante, Anthony S. 1988. *The Facts on File Encyclopedia of World Mythology and Legend*. New York: Facts on File.

Merriam, Alan P. 1964. *The Anthropology of Music*. Evanston, Illinois: Northwestern University Press.

Minsky, Marvin. 1982. "Music, Mind, and Meaning." In *Music, Mind, and Brain: The Neuropsychology of Music*, ed. by Manfred Clynes. New York: Plenum Press.

"Momma Dearest." 1992. *The New Republic*, 10 August, 7.

Montesquieu, Charles. 1989. *The Spirit of the Laws*, trans. and ed. by Anne M. Cohler, Basia Carolyn Miller, and Harold Samuel Stone. Cambridge: Cambridge University Press.

Morris, Christopher. 1967. *Western Political Thought, Volume One: Plato to Augustine*. New York: Basic Books.

Napier, Kristine. 1997. "Antidotes to Pop Culture Poison." *Policy Review*, November-December, 12.

Neely, Kim. 1990. "Rockers Sound Off." *Rolling Stone*, 9 August, 27.

———. 1992. "Record-Chain Blacklist: Superclub Establishes Policy on Rating Lyrics." *Rolling Stone*, 20 August, 18.

Nettleship, Richard Lewis. 1962. *Lectures on the* Republic *of Plato*. New York: St. Martin's Press.

————. 1968. *The Theory of Education in the* Republic *of Plato*. New York: Teachers College Press.

Nichols, Mary. 1987. *Socrates and the Political Community*. Albany: State University of New York Press.

————. 1992. *Citizens and Statesmen: A Study of Aristotle's* Politics. Lanham, Maryland: Rowman and Littlefield.

Nietzsche, Friedrich. 1968a. *Basic Writings of Nietzsche*, trans. and ed. by Walter Kaufmann. New York: The Modern Library.

————. 1968b. *The Will to Power*, trans. by Walter Kaufmann and R.J. Hollingdale. New York: Vintage Books.

————. 1990. *Unmodern Observations*, ed. by William Arrowsmith. New Haven: Yale University Press.

O'Dea, Michael. 1995. *Jean-Jacques Rousseau: Music, Illusion,and Desire*. New York: St. Martin's Press.

Palango, Paul. 1997. "Danger Signs: How One Teen Salvaged Her Life." *Maclean's*, 8 December, 18.

Pangle, Thomas L. 1973. *Montesquieu's Philosophy of Liberalism*. Chicago: University of Chicago Press.

Pattison, Robert. 1987. *The Triumph of Vulgarity: Rock Music in the Mirror of Romanticism*. New York: Oxford University Press.

Plato. 1968. *The Republic of Plato*, trans. by Allan Bloom. New York: Basic Books.

————. 1973. *The Timaeus of Plato*, trans. by R.D. Archer-Hind. New York: Arno Press.

————. 1980. *The Laws of Plato*, trans. by Thomas L. Pangle. New York: Basic Books.

Popper, Karl. 1962. *The Open Society and Its Enemies*, vol. I. Princeton: Princeton University Press.

Pouliot, Janine S. 1998. "The Power of Music." *The World and I*, May, 146.

Ragneskog, Hans, et al. 1996. "Dinner Music for Demented Patients: Analysis of Video-Recorded Observations." *Clinical Nursing Research* 5, no. 3 (August): 262.

Rahe, Paul. 1994a. *Republics Ancient and Modern*, vol. 1, *The Ancien Régime in Classical Greece*. Chapel Hill: University of North Carolina Press.

———. 1994b. *Republics Ancient and Modern*, vol. 2, *New Modes and Orders in Modern Political Thought*. Chapel Hill: University of North Carolina Press.

Rauscher, Frances H., et al. 1993. "Music and Spatial Task Performance." *Nature* 365: 611.

Reibstein, Larry. 1995. "The Right Takes a Media Giant to Task." *Newsweek*, 12 June, 30.

Ressner, Jeffrey. 1991. "To Sticker or Not to Sticker." *Rolling Stone*, 7 February, 17.

Roberts, Johnnie L. 1997. "Music, Money, and Murder: As Rising Body Counts Spur CD Sales, Rap Faces a Crisis." *Newsweek*, 24 March, 76.

"Rock Ratings: An Unnecessary Evil." 1985. *Rolling Stone*, 7 November, 10.

Roederer, Juan G. 1982. "Physical and Neuropsychological Foundations of Music." In *Music, Mind, and Brain: The Neuropsychology of Music*, ed. by Manfred Clynes. New York: Plenum Press, 37-46.

Rouget, Gilbert. 1985. *Music and Trance: A Theory of the Relation Between Music and Possession*, trans. by Brunhilde Biecuyck. Chicago: University of Chicago Press.

Rousseau, Jean-Jacques. 1960. *Politics and the Arts: Letter to M. D'Alembert on the Theatre*, trans. by Allan Bloom. Ithaca, N.Y.: Cornell University Press.

———. 1964. *The First and Second Discourses*, trans. by Roger D. and Judith R. Masters. New York: St. Martin's Press.

———. 1966. *Essay on the Origin of Languages*, trans. by John H. Moran. In *On the Origin of Language*, edited by John H. Moran and Alexander Gode. Chicago: University of Chicago Press.

———. 1975. *A Complete Dictionary of Music*, trans. by William Waring. New York: AMS Press.

Sabine, George H. 1973. *A History of Political Theory*. Hinsdale, Illinois: Dryden Press.

Scott, David. 1996. "Notes for the Alternative Nation." *National Review*, 17 June, 49.

Scott, John. 1995. "Rousseau and the Melodious Language of Freedom." A Paper Prepared for Delivery at the 1995 Annual Meeting of the American Political Science Association, the Chicago Hilton, August 31–September 3, 1995. Copyright by the American Political Science Association.

Shklar, Judith N. 1969. *Men and Citizens: A Study of Rousseau's Social Theory*. Cambridge: Cambridge University Press.

Shreeve, James. 1996. "Music of the Hemispheres: Why Can Toddlers Sing? Why is Even the most Ordinary Human Brain a Library of Melodies?" *Discover*, October, 90.

Sloboda, John A. 1985. *The Musical Mind: The Cognitive Psychology of Music*. Oxford: Clarendon Press.

Smith, Danyel. 1994. "House of Pain." *Rolling Stone*, 7 April, 22.

Stafford, Tim. 1993. "Has Christian Rock Lost its Soul?" *Christianity Today*, 22 November, 14.

Steinberger, Peter J. 1989. "Ruling: Guardians and Philosopher Kings." *American Political Science Review* 83:1207-1225.

Strauss, Leo. 1953. *Natural Right and History*. Chicago: University of Chicago Press.

———. 1959. *What is Political Philosophy?* Chicago: University of Chicago Press.

———. 1964. *The City and Man*. Chicago: University of Chicago Press.

Strauss, Leo, and Joseph Cropsey, eds. 1987. *History of Political Philosophy*, third edition. Chicago: University of Chicago Press.

Strauss, Neil. 1997. "Stage Fright." *Rolling Stone*, 26 June, 19.

Strunk, Oliver, ed. 1950. *Source Readings in Music History: From Classical Antiquity Through the Romantic Era*. New York: W.W. Norton and Company, Inc.

Swanson, Judith A. 1992. *The Public and the Private in Aristotle's Political Philosophy*. Ithaca, N.Y.: Cornell University Press.

Sullivan, Andrew. 1987. "Actually." *The New Republic*, 26 October, 43.

Tanner, Michael. 1994. *Nietzsche*. New York: Oxford University Press.

Teachout, Terry. 1990. "Rap and Racism." Commentary, March, 60-62.

Thigpen, David. 1993. "Restricted Access." *Rolling Stone*, 16 September, 13.

————. 1994. "Up Against the Wall." *Rolling Stone*, 24 February, 16.

Thiele, Leslie Paul. 1990. *Friedrich Nietzsche and the Politics of the Soul.* Princeton: Princeton University Press.

"Tuning up Young Brains." 1994. *Science News*, 27 August, 143.

Verbeke, Gerard. 1990. *Moral Education in Aristotle.* Washington, D.C.: The Catholic University of America Press.

Weinberger, Norman M. 1998. "Brain, Behavior, Biology, and Music: Some Research Findings and their Implications for Educational Policy." *Arts Education Policy Review* 99, no. 3 (January-February): 28.

West, M.L. 1992. *Ancient Greek Music.* Oxford: Clarendon Press.

Westley, Marian, and Ted Gidense. "Music is Good Medicine." *Newsweek*, 21 September, 103.

Wettergreen, John Adams. 1984. "Elements of Ancient and Modern Harmony." In *Natural Right and Political Right*, ed. by Thomas B. Silver and Peter W. Schramm. Durham, North Carolina: Carolina Academic Press, 45-61.

Will, George F. 1983. *Statecraft as Soulcraft.* New York: Simon and Schuster.

Wilson, James Q. 1995. *On Character.* Washington, D.C.: The American Enterprise Institute Press.

Winnington-Ingram, R.P. 1936. *Mode in Ancient Greek Music.* Chicago: Argonaut, Inc., Publishers.

Wokler, Robert. 1995. *Rousseau.* New York: Oxford University Press.

"Women Politicos War on Musical 'Garbage.'" 1993. *Jet*, 6 September, 59.

Young, Julian. 1992. *Nietzsche's Philosophy of Art.* Cambridge: Cambridge University Press.

Zappa, Frank. 1989. "On Junk Food for the Soul." In *Essays on* The Closing of the American Mind, ed. by Robert L. Stone. Chicago: Chicago Review Press, 248.

Zucchino, David. 1985. "Big Brother Meets Twisted Sister." *Rolling Stone*, 7 November, 9.

Index

A NOTE ON THE AUTHOR

CARSON HOLLOWAY teaches political science at Concord College in West Virginia. He holds his doctorate from Northern Illinois University and contributed to *The End of Democracy? II: A Crisis of Legitimacy*, also published by Spence Publishing.

This book was designed and set into type
by Mitchell S. Muncy
and printed and bound
by Thomson-Shore, Inc.,
Dexter, Michigan.

℮

The text face is Minion Multiple Master,
designed by Robert Slimbach
and issued in digital form by Adobe Systems,
Mountain View, California, in 1991.

℮

The cover illustration is *Hot Sax* by Gil Mayers,
reproduced by agreement with SuperStock,
on a cover by Lee Whitmarsh.

℮

The paper is acid-free and is of archival quality.

28